PERSONA

A Style Study
for Readers and Writers

Persona

CONSULTING EDITOR / *Richard Ohmann* / WESLEYAN UNIVERSITY

A STYLE STUDY
FOR READERS
AND WRITERS

by Walker Gibson

University of Massachusetts

 RANDOM HOUSE NEW YORK

Acknowledgments

Acknowledgment is gratefully made to the following authors, agencies, and publishers:

Saul Bellow, selections from *Herzog*. Copyright © 1961, 1963, 1964 by Saul Bellow. All rights reserved. Reprinted by permission of The Viking Press, Inc., and Weidenfeld & Nicolson, Ltd.

The Custom Shop, Shirtmakers, for permission to quote advertising copy.

John Dixon, selections from *Growth Through English*. Reprinted by permission of the Editor of *English in Education*.

First National City Bank, for permission to quote advertising copy.

National Distillers Products Company, for permission to quote advertising copy for Gilbey's Gin.

Newsweek, for permission to quote excerpts from the issue of January 22, 1968.

Ogilvy & Mather Inc., for permission to quote advertising copy for Merrill Lynch.

Father Walter J. Ong, selections from *The Barbarian Within*. Copyright 1962 by the author. Reprinted by permission of The Macmillan Company.

Pan American World Airways, for permission to quote advertising copy.

Dylan Thomas, *Quite Early One Morning*. Copyright 1954 by New Directions Publishing Corporation. "Fern Hill," from *Collected Poems*. Copyright 1952 by Dylan Thomas. Reprinted by permission of New Directions Publishing Corporation, and J. M. Dent and Sons, Ltd., and the Trustees for the Copyrights of the late Dylan Thomas.

The Warner & Swasey Company, for permission to quote advertising copy.

Wells, Rich, Greene Advertising Agency, for permission to quote from a public service ad created for the National Kidney Foundation.

Acting a role, realizing in a specially intense way one's identity (in a sense) with someone who (in another sense) one is not, remains one of the most human things a man can do. WALTER J. ONG

The mask is the face. SUSAN SONTAG

Contents

Contents

Introduction

This is a book for students of reading and writing, students of style. It centers its attention on the author's created *persona*, his mask or voice, in passages of prose. It takes the view that our decisions about the language we use are, in part, calculated to present our reader or listener with a recognizable character who is to do the communicating. If one thinks of Aristotle's three rhetorical means of persuasion—the character of the speaker, the audience, the argument itself—it will be apparent that this book takes its hint from the first of these. But the other two are inevitably involved, in what is a constantly shifting interplay of relationships. Audience and argument affect voice, and the total impact of any communication is surely a more or less indefinable amalgam of all three. In the approach taken here, the message or utterance is seen as modified by the created personality put forth in the act of communicating. In at least some significant ways, the voice, like the medium, *is* the message.

To play a role and don a mask is to raise larger issues of personal identity. Who am I anyway? No teacher can presume to answer that question definitely for a student. But at least it may be possible to suggest some of the ways in which character can be created by words on paper. And it may be that this very concentration on the means by which masks are made is one way to produce *character* in the other sense—a personal identity that is responsible, confident, ready for change. In any event, if this approach does no more than widen for the student his range of stylistic choices and increase his willingness to experiment, it will have satisfied the expectations of *this* book's persona.

Introduction

The first three chapters undertake to identify personas in three familiar kinds of writing: in prose where a first-person-singular speaker introduces himself, in a daily newspaper with its barrage of varied voices, and in a single modern novel. Comparable passages for analysis appear at the end of each of these chapters; these are preceded by some suggestions for practice in creating personas on one's own.

The last three chapters turn more explicitly to the writing process. Chapter 4 speaks of choices in tone—the relation of persona to reader. Chapter 5 speaks of choices in attitude—the relation of persona to subject. The final chapter produces—from sociologists, literary critics, and others—some testimony to the proposition that through role-playing and voice we express our very selves.

A recent Ingmar Bergman film called *Persona* seems to hint at a similar truth. There is something inherently hypocritical in all verbal behavior, in the sense that we are all actors on the stage of the world. Yet to retreat into silence, while it may be honest, is strictly inhuman. Rather, let us play our roles as cheerfully as may be, conscious that they are all we have to offer one another in any search for communion.

I take grateful note here of Richard Ohmann's editorial good advice, and of a remark by Scott Elledge that led me to read *Herzog* as an exercise in voices. For Random House, David Dushkin and Miss Stephanie Wald were helpful and encouraging throughout.

Part I

READING
The Voices We Catch

Chapter 1

Reading the First-Person-Singular

The Latin word *persona* means *mask*—the theatrical mask
that Roman actors wore on the stage, as Greek actors did before
them. Everyone knows the masks of comedy and tragedy still
used for decorations on theatre curtains and proscenium arches.
Actually, there were dozens of such masks in the classical
drama, representing special types of characters; an actor
wearing a particular grimace or furrowed brow or staring eye
could assume that his audience would immediately recognize
him as portraying a particular and familiar type of personality.

Today, in speaking of literary matters, we use the term
persona or *mask* in a slightly different but related sense. Obviously, when an author writes a book he does not literally
wear a mask. In fact, a central difficulty in the experience of
writing is that it happens in isolation from the audience: there
is no one else present to wear a mask *for*. We use the word,
then, in a metaphorical sense—it is as if the author, as he "puts
on his act" for a reader, wore a kind of disguise, taking on, for
a particular purpose, a character who speaks to the reader.
This persona may or may not bear considerable resemblance
to the real author, sitting there at his typewriter; in any case,

the created speaker is certainly less complex than his human inventor. He is inferred entirely out of the language; everything we know about him comes from the words before us on the page. In this respect he is a made man, he is artificial.

It is natural that we should be troubled by expressions like "putting on an act" or "taking on a character." Can't we simply speak and write as ourselves, honestly and candidly? Of course we can, as long as we realize that even our most "honest" acts are indeed acts, in at least two senses of that word. They are acts in the sense that they are forthright and affirmative actions, calculated to bring order into a situation. They are also acts in the sense of playacting, since the means of communication we choose, the roles we play, the language we use, are creative decisions we make, even though we usually make them quite unconsciously. When we call someone a phony or a hypocrite, we usually mean not that he is playing a role, but that he is playing (in our judgment) a wrong role, an inappropriate or misleading one. We make such judgments about people all the time, as we must and should. But we should do so with a vivid sense that in our own performances there is an inevitable element of playacting.

Often persona is used in just that critical sense of hypocrisy or deviousness. It is when we feel that the role being played is obviously affected, or too deliberately self-conscious, or calculated somehow to take us in, that we speak of "so-and-so's persona" almost as a term of abuse.

We spoke above about the inevitable element of playacting in all our performances. Sometimes the very words we use will suggest the double sense of our "acts" of communication: the sense, that is, of serious practical activity combined with role-playing. The word *performance* is an example. We may say that Dean Rusk performed very creditably as Secretary of State, or we may say that Mary Martin performed very creditably in *I Do! I Do!* These are obviously quite different kinds of behavior, but the identical verb suggests that there is something dramatic about all behavior. When you recall that our words *person, personality,* are derived from a Latin word meaning *mask,* you may be given pause about the very identity of your own precious character. And as for *character* itself—we use the word interchangeably for a man's deepest moral qualities and for a role he may play on a stage.

Another term we often use for this "actor" speaking in a piece of literature is, naturally enough, *speaker*, and *the voice of the speaker* is a familiar phrase in literary analysis. But note that this too is metaphorical: there is no literal person speaking, and he has no voice. Nothing is heard. In reading and writing, there are none of those helpful accompaniments we count on in the actual practice of conversing, such as vocal intonation, facial expression, gesture. One of the writer's principal problems is to compensate for these losses, for most people are more convincing in person than on paper. That is why writing has to be learned; that is why books like this one are offered as helps for writers. Somehow the writer has to evoke, out of mere ink marks on paper, a character whose language the reader will trust, enjoy, profit from.

Sometimes, especially in our own time, a writer performs his act by endeavoring to put on paper the words and rhythms of actual conversation, as realistically as he can. He tries, in other words, to break the barrier between spoken and written language; he tries to write like a talker. This is particularly true of some modern fiction. Take an obvious example, from the work of J. D. Salinger. Everyone knows the novel that opens with these words:

> If you really want to hear about it, the first thing you'll probably want to know is where I was born, and what my lousy childhood was like, and how my parents were occupied and all before they had me, and all that David Copperfield kind of crap, but I don't feel like going into it, if you want to know the truth. In the first place, that stuff bores me, and in the second place, my parents would have two hemorrhages apiece if I told anything pretty personal about them.

Mr. Salinger was of course no teenager when he wrote *The Catcher in the Rye*, but for his particular purpose he took on a teenaged persona, naming him, you remember, Holden Caulfield. Here we have Holden beginning to tell the story of his recent adventures—and the word *tell* is appropriate. We are to share in the illusion that this story was not written at all—as if we were somehow overhearing someone talking to us. It is as if

5

Holden had told the story to someone who had a tape recorder, and his talk was later printed up from the recording.

How do we decide, as readers, that the voice we are aware of here is more that of a teenager-*talker* than that of a *writer*? First, there is the simple matter of vocabulary: you notice words and phrases that are more familiar when listening to people talking than when reading what people write. "My lousy childhood," or "that kind of crap," or "that stuff bores me." Such expressions, in print, may be commonplace inside quotation marks, as parts of a conversation, but here the entire discourse seems part of a conversation. In the first sentence, Holden begins by referring to us, the listener. "If you really want to hear about it . . ." And what is this "it" he mentions? It is what happened to him, but we have to guess that, for Holden doesn't try to explain. When we talk to someone we take a lot for granted, as Holden does here. It is as if we knew him before we opened the book; as if a dialogue had already been going on, which the first page only continues—but from here on we hear only one side of this dialogue.

A careful reader will be conscious of other details in the language that are calculated to put before him the persona of a teenager talking. Holden uses contractions ("you'll," "don't") as one does in speech. His sentences meander in a loose sort of structure. And he exaggerates in what we recognize as a particularly youthful way—"two hemorrhages apiece."

We have stated that this practice of creating a conversational voice may be especially noticeable in the fiction of our own time, but actually Holden's voice has distinguished forbears. Here is an even more familiar author, of a hundred years ago, also adopting the role of a teenager, though the expression *teenager* would have seemed to him very strange.

You don't know about me, without you have read a book by the name of *The Adventures of Tom Sawyer,* but that ain't no matter. That book was made by Mr. Mark Twain, and he told the truth, mainly. There was things he stretched, but mainly he told the truth.

Again, the details that alert the reader to the presence of Huckleberry Finn are obvious enough. The word "without" in the first line will suffice for comment. Used for "unless," it is of course colloquial. It is also regional, not to be found everywhere in the

6

United States, and perhaps hardly at all elsewhere in the English-speaking world. This usage is also dated, though still present in some communities. Even if we did not know when the book was written, or when the "telling" was supposed to be taking place, we could reasonably guess that it was some time ago simply on the basis of this archaic use of "without."

But, obviously, not all first-person-singular narrators beginning tales of their own lives project before us a loose-talking conversationalist of the Huck and Holden kind. In fact, Mark Twain and Salinger would not have written the way they did if it were not for the existence of a traditional way of telling one's own story that implies a voice of a very different kind. They both deliberately departed from a "norm," a "proper" style for such personal accounts. Suppose we look at a version of such a norm in the very work so deprecatingly alluded to by Holden Caulfield. Here is the way David Copperfield begins his story:

> Whether I shall turn out to be the hero of my own life, or whether that station will be held by anybody else, these pages must show. To begin my life with the beginning of my life, I record that I was born . . .

What can you see in these words that you would be unlikely to hear someone say aloud to someone else? The vocabulary is not at all abstruse, though "that station" is probably an expression you would be unlikely to hear someone utter aloud with that meaning. More to the point is the way the whole first sentence is put together. It begins with two fairly lengthy subordinate clauses, balanced in what we call parallel structure. Very few people can talk this way. The sentence is so neatly organized that it looks as though someone had figured it out carefully beforehand. One can write this way; only rather literary people talk this way. This persona, then, is first a more literary kind of fellow. We should note, too, his sophisticated wittiness, as in the playing with the word "life" in the second sentence. How does that pun affect the way we respond to this fellow?

We can see, then, a general distinction as to the persona an author may choose. He can sound like a talker, or he can sound like a writer. A damaging characteristic of much amateur writing lies precisely here: the voice may sound like both talker and writer at the same time. The persona, that is, emerges as double, a split personality. Such a muddle can succeed in certain kinds of rather fancy literature, as we shall see, but only when the author is well aware of what he is doing.

We can try to clarify this distinction between talking-style and writing-style by revising the examples we have already looked at. Suppose we try to make Holden Caulfield sound like a writer rather than a talker. (We will absolutely ruin him, of course, in the process.) Here is the beginning of that first sentence again:

> If you really want to hear about it, the first thing you'll probably want to know is where I was born, and what my lousy childhood was like, and how my parents were occupied and all before they had me . . .

It would not be difficult to take the general meaning of Holden's message and translate it into a style that would sound more traditionally bookish, more like a writer-persona. For instance, one could rewrite those *where, what,* and *how* clauses into phrases more closely parallel, more precisely balanced:

> The place of my birth, the nature of my childhood, the occupations of my parents—these are no doubt pieces of information you will want to be given.

In writing such a version, we change "you'll" to "you will," and "thing" to "pieces of information." A passive infinitive concludes the sentence. And the order of parts, the elaborate trio of noun phrases at the start, is simply not the sort of thing people find congenial or even possible in their ordinary talk.

The noun phrases themselves deserve further comment. When you change a clause with its independent verb ("where I was born") into a noun phrase ("the place of my birth"), you have changed your mask from talker to writer, or at least you are moving in that direction. It is by such choices that a persona is made. Indeed, most informal-colloquial voices will display a relatively high proportion of independent verbs, perhaps one for every seven or eight words. On the other hand, most formal-literary voices use far fewer such verbs, perhaps as few as one for every twenty or twenty-five words. Notice that in the revision of

Holden's sentence the number of independent verbs has been reduced from six to two.

Suppose we try a similar transformation upon the character of Huck Finn, this time without reducing the proportion of verbs. Here is his first sentence again:

> You don't know about me, without you have read a book by the name of *The Adventures of Tom Sawyer*, but that ain't no matter.

We can make Huck a little older and more educated, a writer rather than a talker, by simple changes in the vocabulary and in the arrangement of parts. We begin with a subordinate clause.

> Unless you have perused the volume entitled *The Adventures of Tom Sawyer*, you can have little knowledge of me, but that is of small consequence.

A reverse process can be applied to the opening lines of *David Copperfield*, in which the traditional, formal-literary voice becomes a loose, idiomatic, contemporary talker:

> I don't know whether I'll be the hero of this story or not—maybe somebody else will.

Here one of our changes has to do again with subordination: the clause follows the main subject-verb pattern, rather than preceding it as in the original. Other details should be obvious: the substitution of "will" for "shall," the use of contractions, the higher proportion of verbs.

These alterations of persona will suggest that there are specific rhetorical "tricks" one can perform to change the character of one's stylistic mask. By and large this is true. But one must beware of making such tricks into too easy a formula. It is generally true that a subordinate clause placed *before* the main subject-verb, rather than after it, will tend to make the voice more literary and formal. But notice that Holden Caulfield's original first sentence actually begins with such a clause ("If you really want to know about it . . ."). In Holden's case, of course, the effect of this placement of the clause is more than compensated for by his other colloquial weapons.

On the next few pages you will find a series of short opening passages from works in which a first-person-singular speaker begins an account of his early life. Some of these manifest formal voices that make no bones about being bookish and literary; others approach the styles of conversation. Do not be misled into assuming that this is simply a chronological development, and that all works of the past are formal-literary while modern authors are uniformly loose and colloquial. Both the first two passages in this series are from the eighteenth century, and both rather loosely organized; one is sober and informative, while the other is an exuberant echo of off-the-cuff monologue. The most bewilderingly mixed voice in this collection is also the most recent (from John Barth's *Giles Goat-Boy*); in this work formal, stylized effects go hand in hand with highly colloquial phrasing, jokes, asides, and so on. This is the deliberate muddle of writer-style and talker-style in some modern literature alluded to above.

§ Assessing each of these passages, the student of style might profitably ask himself: Is the voice I hear in these sentences primarily a writer's voice, or a talker's? How am I being asked to respond to this persona—are we friendly and intimate, or distant and unsociable? Most important: According to what details of vocabulary and sentence structure do I make these judgments?

§ The student who enjoys playing games with style may want to go further and actually manipulate the language so as to produce a persona radically different from the one the author created. As we did earlier with passages from Salinger, Mark Twain, and Dickens, one can always alter sentence structure and diction to create another voice altogether. Authors may writhe in their graves as we do this, but the lesson to be learned—the power of language in creating a persona—should be worth the risk of blasphemy.

§ Still a further question will occur to the thoughtful student: What is the relation of the created "I" to the actual personality of the author himself? In most of these passages the "I" is frankly fictitious, a made-up person whom the reader is expected to recognize as decidedly distinct from the author. Generally, these are not autobiographies (though selection 5 is playfully called an autobiography). The people talking here are no more synonymous with their authors than Huck Finn was with Mark Twain. The last three passages in the collection, however, pose a different problem. These three *are* autobiographical—they are all reminiscences of childhood—and they are all by the same author, Dylan Thomas. Thomas was a man with a very distinctive style and voice; as a writer he created a persona more uniform and unique to himself than do most writers. Still, in these three passages he speaks to us in clearly different voices. In one he is almost chatty, in the second he is intense and lyrical, more aggressively metaphorical, while in the third (to be sure it is a poem) he is very intense indeed. Like all authors, Thomas took on different voices for different literary situations, even when the subject matter, his own childhood, was virtually the same. There is a phonograph record (Caedmon TC 1002) in which Thomas reads the second and third of our three selections, and a careful hearing of that record will show how, in his reading, Thomas used his own literal voice somewhat differently to distinguish between two of his many styles.

The fact is, as we shall see in later chapters, it is impossible to speak of oneself, or indeed of anything, without some kind of dramatic role-playing, some assumption of a persona. Our task, recognizing this, is to choose with some awareness of possibilities and alternatives, to choose responsibly, flexibly, and consciously.

1

I was born in the year 1632, in the city of York, of a good family, though not of that country, my father being a foreigner of Bremen, who settled first at Hull; he got a good estate by merchandise, and leaving off his trade, lived afterward at York; from whence he had married my mother, whose relations were named Robinson, a very good family in that country, and from whom I was called Robinson Kreutznaer; but, by the usual corruption of words in England, we are now called, nay, we call ourselves, Crusoe; and so my companions always called me.

I had two elder brothers, one of whom was lieutenant-colonel to an English regiment of foot in Flanders, formerly commanded by the famous Colonel Lockhart, and was killed at the battle near Dunkirk against the Spaniards. What became of my second brother I never knew, any more than my father or mother did know what was become of me.*

* Identifications of these numbered passages appear at the back of the book under Sources of Quoted Passages and Notes.

2

I wish either my father or my mother, or indeed both of them, as they were in duty both equally bound to it, had minded what they were about when they begot me; had they duly considered how much depended upon what they were then doing;—that not only the production of a rational Being was concerned in it, but that possibly the happy formation and temperature of his body, perhaps his genius and the very cast of his mind;—and, for all they knew to the contrary, even the fortunes of his whole house might take their turn from the humours and dispositions which were then uppermost;——Had they duly weighed and considered all this, and proceeded accordingly,——I am verily persuaded I should have made a quite different figure in the world, from that in which the reader is likely to see me.—Believe me, good folks, this is not so inconsiderable a thing as many of you may think it;—you have all, I dare say, heard of the animal spirits, as how they are transfused from father to son etc. etc.—and a great deal to that purpose:—Well, you may take my word, that nine parts in ten of a man's sense or his nonsense, his successes and miscarriages in this world depend upon their motions and activity, and the different tracts and trains you put them into, so that when they are once set a-going, whether right or wrong, 'tis not a halfpenny matter,—away they go cluttering like hey-go mad; and by treading the same steps over and over again, they presently make a road of it, as plain and as smooth as a garden-walk, which, when they are once used to, the Devil himself sometimes shall not be able to drive them off it.

3

When I was a small boy at the beginning of the century I remember an old man who wore knee-breeches and worsted stockings, and who used to hobble about the street of our village with the help of a stick. He must have been getting on for eighty in the year 1807, earlier than which date I suppose I can hardly remember him, for I was born in 1802. A few white locks hung about his ears, his shoulders were bent and his knees feeble, but he was still hale, and was much respected in our little world of Paleham. His name was Pontifex.

His wife was said to be his master; I have been told she brought him a little money, but it cannot have been much. She was a tall, square-shouldered person (I have heard my father call her a Gothic woman) who had insisted on being married to Mr. Pontifex when he was young and too good-natured to say nay to any woman who wooed him. The pair had lived not unhappily together, for Mr. Pontifex's temper was easy and he soon learned to bow before his wife's more stormy moods.

4

I am an American. I was born and reared in Hartford, in the state of Connecticut—anyway, just over the river, in the country. So I am a Yankee of the Yankees—and practical; yes, and nearly barren of sentiment, I suppose—or poetry, in other words. My father was a blacksmith, my uncle was a horse doctor, and I was both, along at first. Then I went over to the great arms factory and learned my real trade; learned all there was to it; learned to make everything: guns, revolvers, cannon, boilers, anything a body wanted—anything in the world, it didn't make any difference what; and if there wasn't any quick newfangled way to make a thing, I could invent one—and do it as easy as rolling off a log. I became head superintendent; had a couple of thousand men under me.

Well, a man like that is a man that is full of fight—that goes without saying. With a couple of thousand rough men under one, one has plenty of that sort of amusement. I had, anyway. At last I met my match, and I got my dose. It was during a misunderstanding conducted with crowbars with a fellow we used to call Hercules. He laid me out with a crusher alongside the head that made everything crack, and seemed to spring every joint in my skull and made it overlap its neighbor. Then the world went out in darkness, and I didn't feel anything more, and didn't know anything at all—at least for a while.

5

I was born in San Francisco, California. I have in consequence always preferred living in a temperate climate, but it is difficult, on the continent of Europe or even in America, to find a temperate climate and live in it. My mother's father was a pioneer, he came to California in '49, he married my grandmother who was very fond of music. She was a pupil of Clara Schumann's father. My mother was a quiet charming woman named Emilie.

My father came of polish patriotic stock. His grand-uncle raised a regiment for Napoleon and was its colonel. His father left his mother just after their marriage, to fight at the barricades in Paris, but his wife having cut off his supplies, he soon returned and led the life of a conservative well to do land owner.

13

6

I am an American, Chicago born—Chicago, that somber city—and go at things as I have taught myself, free-style, and will make the record in my own way: first to knock, first admitted; sometimes an innocent knock, sometimes a not so innocent. But a man's character is his fate, says Heraclitus, and in the end there isn't any way to disguise the nature of the knocks by acoustical work on the door or gloving the knuckles.

Everybody knows there is no fineness or accuracy of suppression; if you hold down one thing you hold down the adjoining.

My own parents were not much to me, though I cared for my mother. She was simple-minded, and what I learned from her was not what she taught, but on the order of object lessons. She didn't have much to teach, poor woman.

7

I first met Dean not long after my wife and I split up. I had just gotten over a serious illness that I won't bother to talk about, except that it had something to do with the miserably weary split-up and my feeling that everything was dead. With the coming of Dean Moriarty began the part of my life you could call my life on the road. Before that I'd often dreamed of going West to see the country, always vaguely planning and never taking off. Dean is the perfect guy for the road because he actually was born on the road, when his parents were passing through Salt Lake City in 1926, in a jalopy, on their way to Los Angeles. First reports of him came to me through Chad King, who'd shown me a few letters from him written in a New Mexico reform school. I was tremendously interested in the letters because they so naïvely and sweetly asked Chad to teach him all about Nietzsche and all the wonderful intellectual things that Chad knew. At one point Carlo and I talked about the letters and wondered if we would ever meet the strange Dean Moriarty. This is all far back, when Dean was not the way he is today, when he was a young jailkid shrouded in mystery. Then news came that Dean was out of reform school and was coming to New York for the first time; also there was talk that he had just married a girl called Marylou.

8

If I ever sit down like a retired Scotland Yard inspector to write my memoirs, which I have provisionally entitled "Forty Years a Boob," one of the episodes I plan to gloze over is the night of pub-crawling I spent in Hollywood last summer with a beautiful Amazonian extra player named, for the purposes of this indiscretion, Audrey Merridew. For nine tumultuous hours, her destiny and mine were interwoven. (No more than our destinies, I hasten to add; we never even progressed to the point of lacing fingers.) The encounter was so brief, our lack of rapport so conclusive, that when I received a postcard from her recently—an aerial view of San Bernardino, with a tiny shrunken lemon wired to it—I could not recall the creature for a few seconds. Then the whole gruesome affair came back, and I realized with an uprush of pique that the card had an ulterior significance. So I was a wizened little fruit long past its prime, was I? That was feminine gratitude for you; you danced attendance on them, flattered their vanity, listened to their preposterous confidences, subordinated everything to their whims, and in return they made you a laughing stock across the country. Standing at my rural-delivery box in the Pennsylvania bush, I could hear the personnel of the entire postal system, from coast to coast, guffawing at the gibe. Well, I thought, it's damn lucky a continent lies between us, or I'd hang a shiner on Audrey's eye, for all the eight inches she towers over me. When my dander's up, I lash out irrespective of size or sex.

9

George is my name; my deeds have been heard of in Tower Hall, and my childhood has been chronicled in the *Journal of Experimental Psychology*. I am he that was called in those days Billy Bocksfuss— cruel misnomer. For had I indeed a cloven foot I'd not now hobble upon a stick or need ride pick-a-back to class in humid weather. Aye, it was just for want of a proper hoof that in my fourteenth year I was the kicked instead of the kicker; that I lay crippled on the reeking peat and saw my first love tupped by a brute Angora. Mercy on the buck who butted me from one world to another; whose fell horns turned by sweetheart's fancy, drove me from the pasture, and set me gimping down the road I travel yet. This bare brow, shame of my kidship, he crowned with the same of men: I bade farewell to my hornless goathood and stuck out, a hornèd human student, for Commencement Gate.

I was, in other words, the Ag-Hill Goat-Boy. Who misbegot me, and on whom, who knew, or in what corner of the University I drew first breath? It was my fate to call no man Daddy, no woman Mom.

15

10

I like very much people telling me about their childhood, but they'll have to be quick or else I'll be telling them about mine.

I was born in a large Welsh town at the beginning of the Great War—an ugly, lovely town (or so it was and is to me), crawling, sprawling by a long and splendid curving shore where truant boys and sandfield boys and old men from nowhere, beachcombed, idled and paddled, watched the dock-bound ships or the ships steaming away into wonder and India, magic and China, countries bright with oranges and loud with lions; threw stones into the sea for the barking outcast dogs; made castles and forts and harbours and race tracks in the sand; and on Saturday summer afternoons listened to the brass band, watched the Punch and Judy, or hung about on the fringes of the crowd to hear the fierce religious speakers who shouted to the sea, as though it were wicked and wrong to roll in and out like that, white-horsed and full of fishes.

11

One Christmas was so much like another, in those years around the sea-town corner now and out of all sound except the distant speaking of the voices I sometimes hear a moment before sleep, that I can never remember whether it snowed for six days and six nights when I was twelve or whether it snowed for twelve days and twelve nights when I was six. All the Christmases roll down toward the two-tongued sea, like a cold and headlong moon bundling down the sky that was our street; and they stop at the rim of the ice-edged, fish-freezing waves, and I plunge my hands in the snow and bring out whatever I can find. In goes my hand into that wool-white bell-tongued ball of holidays resting at the rim of the carol-singing sea. and out come Mrs. Prothero and the firemen.

12

Now as I was young and easy under the apple boughs
About the lilting house and happy as the grass was green,
   The night above the dingle starry,
    Time let me hail and climb
   Golden in the heydays of his eyes,
And honoured among wagons I was prince of the apple towns
And once below a time I lordly had the trees and leaves
   Trail with daisies and barley
   Down the rivers of the windfall light.

16

Reading the First-Person-Singular

And as I was green and carefree, famous among the barns
About the happy yard and singing as the farm was home,
   In the sun that is young once only,
     Time let me play and be
   Golden in the mercy of his means,
And green and golden I was huntsman and herdsman, the calves
Sang to my horn, the foxes on the hills barked clear and cold,
    And the sabbath rang slowly
   In the pebbles of the holy streams.

Chapter 2

Reading the News

So far we have been considering situations in which a writer projects upon his reader an explicit "I," a person talking. This "I" may be candidly fictitious, like Huck Finn, or he may purport to speak for the author himself, like the several voices of Dylan Thomas. In either case, there is some sort of play-acting taking place, some effort to pose as a particular character for a particular purpose. Obviously, in all these first-person-singular situations, the persona is for the reader a character to be reckoned with.

But what about the more common situations in prose, where there is no explicit "I"? What about "objective" writing, as in good news reporting? What about legal documents, math textbooks, committee reports? What about all the writing we see that is deliberately impersonal?

The answer is that there is always an "I," whether he is expressed or not. There is always a character speaking, a voice we are asked to tune in to, even though, in much writing, we may have little to say about its quality and tone. In some writing, let us cheerfully concede, an analysis through persona or voice may simply be not particularly interesting or appropriate. In "straight" news reporting, for example, the speaker may be characterized chiefly by his eagerness not to be seen, his energy in backing out of the picture. A voice can be faceless. It is as if the persona were saying, "I'm just a middleman here, I'm just telling you what I've been told, without comment. I am a colorless recording machine."

The Johnson Administration deplored Israel's annexation of Old Jerusalem today as a hasty and unilateral move that the United States could not recognize as valid.

Moreover, President Johnson left the impression that he felt that the Israeli leaders had upset his confidence in their "wisdom and good judgment."

Apparently they acted before receiving word of a last-minute public plea by the President for world-wide consultation on the problem. But they had ample indication of the American view, officials said.

Notice what a different effect this passage would have if the last two words were removed. "They had ample indication of the American view." In that case, the persona becomes a critical and knowledgeable fellow who leaves the Israelis with little excuse for their action. *He* decides how much "indication" is "ample." As the passage stands, however, the persona is hardly involved at all; he merely paraphrases for us what certain (unnamed) "officials said." Notice the qualifying adverb "apparently" at the beginning of his third paragraph—our friend is not going to be caught making this assertion as a certain truth. This is a very cautious mask, revealing little of the human being behind it. (A most difficult role to play in real life!) Perhaps all we can say about the character of this speaker is that he is the sort of serious person who assumes that information like that he is presenting will, or should, interest and concern us.

Many other possible voices might have been employed to convey this information, though it would hardly be the same information if uttered by a different persona in a different style of expression. One might imagine the voice of a loyal Arab or Israeli, or that of a historian, or a military expert. In the same issue of the newspaper where the quoted report appears on page 1 (this happens to be *The New York Times* for June 29, 1967), the persona of the editorial page has this to say:

Following its success in a blitz war, Israel has now taken a step toward a blitz peace with the abrupt annexation of Jerusalem's captured Old City. But lasting peace cannot be won this way.

Far from merely paraphrasing the accounts of others, this persona takes a firm, authoritarian attitude. He knows! The value judgments he expresses are partly revealed through adjectives. When you coin the phrase "blitz peace," you are probably against it; it is doubtful that an Israeli would describe the situation in that way. To call the annexation "abrupt" is to suggest that it was unjustifiably so. Other expressions that another kind of voice might have used, revealing different values, might be *efficient,* or *well-planned,* or even *necessary.* These are honorific adjectives, giving a favorable interpretation of the modified noun. "Abrupt" and "blitz," in the context of the editorial, are pejorative: they color the situation in an unfavorable light. We will be saying more about the way adjectives and other parts of speech are used to express value judgments when we confront problems of attitude in Chapter 5.

It is interesting that in actual fact the Israelis very soon had to face squarely what words they would use to describe their action in Jerusalem. The following day's *Times* carried an account of a news conference with Foreign Minister Abba Eban, in which this official rejected the notion that the word "annexation" was appropriate. He had a very different way of describing the whole situation. "Mr. Eban, asked at a news conference whether Israel had 'annexed' Jerusalem, said that he preferred to use his own vocabulary. He repeated this reply when asked whether Jerusalem was not part of Israel. The policy of the Israeli Government, he said later in an explanatory statement, was to promote and maintain the unity of Jerusalem, to elevate its cultural and social standards and to protect the holy places." Semantic gamesmanship, as played by high dignitaries of state, should provide the student with continuous instruction, not to say amusement. Question: Was or was not Old Jerusalem annexed? Answer: What does "annexed" mean? Or rather: Who's talking?

The variety of voices present in any morning newspaper is almost bewildering, even in a staid and responsible publication like the one in hand. Turning back to page 1 of our June 29 issue, we find there a sort of "background article" on Indonesia, in which the correspondent is at liberty to make far more sweeping statements than the cautious reporter of the Israeli item.

Having lived in the turbulence of "unfinished revolution" for more than 20 years, Indonesia is adjusting slowly and painfully to a quieter climate of pragmatic evolution.

Here the evidence that Indonesia is adjusting as claimed will presumably be forthcoming in the article. But the conclusion with which the article begins is the author's own; *he* has made a judgment from the evidence, and he is by no means confined to simply reporting the opinions of others. Consequently the persona we are introduced to here is assured and informed, in command. He even permits himself a turn of phrase almost witty— "revolution" and "evolution."

Sometimes the *Times* and other newspapers appear to signal the entrance of a more free-wheeling speaking voice by typographical means—that is, by changing the type-face of the headline. A headline printed in italics can prepare the alert reader for a persona less cautious and detached. The formal Roman capitals, on the other hand, usually suggest the almost faceless mask of that reporter-repeater who told us of Jerusalem's annexation.

In any case a newspaper's voice is not a single note. It varies constantly—as it should, of course—from item to item, as the writers face different problems, follow different instructions from their editors, and in the process assume different relations with the reader. Of course the reader is all one person—you or I— though we too take on different roles as we expose ourselves to different voices. We are not quite the same character ourselves as we read a news column, an editorial, an ad. The assumptions we are asked to share force us to alter our reading self from column to column. Thus when we say, facing a formidable report on economic policy, that we "aren't in the mood for that," we mean simply that we are not at present willing to become the reading character that the particular document demands.

In many parts of the paper—book and movie reviews, sports pages—the writer is permitted, indeed encouraged, to take on personal color and tone, and the reader relaxes accordingly. The speaker may even display some of the rhetoric of the talker that we observed in the previous chapter. Here is a movie reviewer who takes on the role of a witty, discriminating, rather superior person, sharing with us, the reader, a lofty view of standard television entertainment but willing to use the colloquial language too. Note how, if we are to read sympathetically, we must take on some of his characteristics and attitudes ourselves.

"GUNN" is slick proof that the unblinking private eye of the title, who already has dispatched hundreds of hard guys in a thousand and one nights of half-hour fictions, is equally indestructible in a film running an hour and a half. It opened yesterday at the Forum and 68th Street Playhouse. Blake Edwards, who created him, has merely made him larger than life. There are enough shootings, girls and corpses to satisfy the bloodthirsty and the girl-watchers, but aside from a hip script and a weird, gory, slightly unexpected climax, "Gunn" really has never left the television screen.

Much of the effect here is gained by the use of tired old clichés that we are expected to recognize and laugh at as the speaker does. "Private eye," "hard guys," "a thousand and one nights," "larger than life"—such phrases are reminders to us of the tired quality of the film under discussion. Moreover the speaker uses them wittily in combinations. When he says "hundreds of hard guys in a thousand and one nights," we are to understand that he is ludicrously putting together a phrase from whodunit literature and a phrase from traditional literature in a juxtaposition perhaps never before uttered. When he says "hard," we are to understand that the guys aren't believably hard at all, they're monotonous and predictable. And when he says "a thousand and one nights," we know that he means not the romantic tales of *The Arabian Nights* (though we are to recognize and appreciate the allusion) —he means instead, quite literally, years of deadly-dull evening TV shows. The persona, sharing all these little jokes with his reader, is of course far closer to the reader than was the case with the news and editorial voices we have so far observed.

One of the pleasures of newspaper reading is that the dignity, and the pretension, of the voices in the news columns and editorials are constantly being undercut by other voices. The most spectacular are the cheerful cries of the admen. Here are some samples, from the same issue of the *Times:*

Reading the News

1

You'll never read a book with greater interest. Earn 5% on your savings with our Golden Passbook Account.

2

Amsterdam is a whole lot more than charming canals and historic houses. There, by the beautiful zee, you can watch diamonds being cut, and do some cutting up of your own in some of Europe's sassiest cabarets.

3

Break out the frosty bottle, boys, and keep your collins dry!

4

Do you know which collar style suits *you* best? For example, do you need a lower collar? a higher collar? a quarter size collar? Perhaps you want a tapered waistline, or even, an in-between sleeve length.

A good deal of solemn sermonizing has no doubt come your way about the immorality of advertising, how it creates unnecessary desires, employs illogical arguments, and generally abuses good sense. Maybe so. But as students of style, suppose we take another approach. The best protection against the appeals of advertising is not an entrenched hostility to all its forms, but instead some understanding of the rhetorical techniques by which it is constructed. In the case of many contemporary ads, a crucial aspect of the rhetoric is a certain play of wit in manipulating clichés. The adman takes a familiar phrase in current use, and by slightly altering its language or meaning he provokes in us a slight smile, and, he hopes, a favorable attitude toward himself and his product. "You'll never read a book with greater interest." How many times have we heard that tired sentence? If this were an ad for a new bestseller, it would be a terrible bore. When someone talks to us like that about a book, we're likely *not* to read the book simply because anyone who speaks in that all-too-commonplace way can't really be a very discriminating source of advice. But the ad in question (see 1 above) is not, of course, an ad for a publisher at all, it is an ad for a bank. We experience a slight double take with the word "book," for this is not a book one reads, but a bankbook! Then, when we appreciate the further pun on the word "interest," we can see at least that the ad writer has his wits about him. We may not be persuaded that a Golden Passbook Account is a good thing to have, but we *can* be persuaded that the persona here is not a fool. There is no law against simply enjoying hopped-up language like this. On the other hand, you may prefer to label the voice that of a cheap punster, far too palsy for comfort.

Puns may be, as is so often urged, the lowest form of humor, but their presence in much advertising should remind us that the reading of ads need be no solemn affair. "You can watch diamonds being cut, or do some cutting up of your own." Not the best joke you ever heard? True, but it is a joke. Sometimes a jocular allusion in an ad can be suggested by moderately subtle means, with echoes of words and rhythm, as in 3, an ad for Gilbey's Gin. "Break out the frosty bottle, boys, and keep your collins dry!" We may or may not recall the precise source here—Valentine Blacker's *Oliver's Advice* (1834)—and that the original line went "Put your trust in God, my boys, and keep your powder dry." But we certainly have a sense of that source as a rollicking piece of religio-military heroism, familiar to the ear. At the same time there is surely some irony in the echo. It is absurd to connect a grand old heroic sentiment with the drinking of gin! This absurdity is part of the fun in the ad too; we do not lose sympathy with the speaker when we recognize that he may be laughing at himself.

Throughout all advertising, whether jocular or not, there is an effort to buttonhole the reader by uses of language that promote a close relation with the speaker. The most obvious device in this direction is simple enough: the second person pronoun. Note in all our examples the repetitions of "you," "your," as well as the direct appeal of the imperative voice ("break out," "keep"). In example 4 above, the stress on "your" particular needs may be intended as especially flattering. In addition, observe those familiar devices of language that once again create the persona as an easy-going talker-fellow rather than as a writer-fellow. Contractions: "you'll never read." Colloquialisms: "cutting up," "sassiest." The list of short fragmented questions familiar in speech: "a higher collar?" "a quarter size collar?"

24

Leafing on through our paper, we come to the sports pages, and as we do so we feel that familiar lift from our shoulders of whatever burden of responsibility we may have experienced reading the solemn reports from Jerusalem. We do not even have to keep our hands clutched to our wallets, as we must while reading the ads. The sportswriter, more than any other reporter of news, is free to kid around, cozy up to the reader, and employ the rhetoric of oral speech. Here is an excerpt from a report from Henley-on-Thames, England, where some crew races were taking place.

Cornell is one of the major attractions here. . . . Eleven days ago, it lost by only four lengths in Germany to Ratzeburg's world champions, a notable feat for a lightweight crew against heavyweights.

Lightweight, well, sort of. At home, this Cornell boat could average no more than 155 pounds, and no man could exceed 160. But there is no weight restriction here, and Cornell has been eating.

It now averages almost 170 pounds. Dennis Koza, of Roselle Park, N.J., the 6-foot-3 inch captain, is up to 178.

Cornell was in the boathouse by noon. Others weren't so lucky. From 9:45 A.M. to 7 P.M., a race started every five or 10 minutes— sort of a Penn Relays on water. It was a long day.

"By the time they run the last race," said a wise old oar, "all but the connoisseurs will be firmly entrenched in the bars."

All were, including the wise old oar.

Are we not invited by this genial persona to assume that, standing next to the wise old oar, also firmly entrenched, was the writer himself?

The sportswriter at his best can be not only gay and genial, but adept with lively phrases and original metaphors. At his worst he becomes a mere shuffler of overused synonyms. See your own campus newspaper, where the coach is always a mentor, a team is an aggregation, and close games are invariably won by slim margins. We may properly feel personally insulted at such monotony, for the inference is that we are informed and entertained by dreariness, and to so suggest is to demean us.

How can the student of style increase the pleasure and profit he derives from the reading of the news? One thing to do, of course, is to pick up today's paper—any paper—and examine its various columns for a barrage of different personas. A cacophony of voices. What sort of character expresses the social news; who describes a marriage ceremony? Who intones the obituary? What is the voice of the woman's page, with its tidings of food and furniture? What about the letters to the editor? The financial news? It is a rich hunting ground, one in which the assumptions that a reader is expected to take on can vary with every turn of the eye.

§ Still another, more energetic, exercise for the student of style is this: write your own newspaper. Not a full 80-page issue, of course, but a sampler of styles in imitation of the newspaper's varied personas. You might include at least the following: a paragraph of international political news, a dispatch from a war zone, a page-one item about a famous figure's divorce, another about a famous figure's death, an editorial deploring the divorce and one praising the deceased, a letter or two, some sports news, a column on women's fashions, a review of a new TV program, and several ads. When you have finished, you may not have a product ready to be hawked at a newsstand, but you should know a little more about the chorus of voices that purport to give us the day's happenings. A newspaper is, in another sense, a "happening"—a montage of conflicting experiences crying for attention in disparate styles.

§ If this exercise in literary role-playing bears fruit, it might be enlightening to try a somewhat similar effort with another great medium of our time, television. Turn on your screen for an hour, but keep the audio silent. Taking your cues from the faces and expressions on the screen, make up appropriate sentences and try uttering them in appropriate tones of voice. Again, the general experience should be one of topsy-turvy variety: the public figure making his portentous statement, the newscaster, the Dodge rebellion girl (she wants *you*), and so on. Not everyone is gifted at this sort of performance, but the practice ought to be wholesome even for the most inarticulate of us. Many of us are "voicebound," in the sense that nonathletic people are musclebound. Try a few voices on, for size.

§ Still another exercise in the creating of voices is one that has become familiar in British schools, the writing of scripts. You could try composing a dialogue between two or more characters, each of whom is consistently distinguishable by his language and style. Some examples: a college dean and an advocate of student power; a gas station attendant and the driver of a Sting Ray; a football coach and an English teacher. Think of these as scripts for radio rather than TV, so that your individuals become distinct from one another solely by what they say and the way they say it.

§ Finally, here is a somewhat different version of the news. The following passages are from a single issue of *Newsweek* magazine (January 22, 1968), and they present not so much a cacophony of contradictory voices as varieties of a single voice. It may be that people who buy and read a newsmagazine are unconsciously seeking just that: the mysteries of the day explained by one, strong, confident, sophisticated, wisecracking, singleminded, ever-so-up-to-date and knowledgeable character. In any case, look at these passages with such a possibility in mind. Perhaps even the ads share some qualities with *Newsweek*'s editorial persona. (The last three quotations are ads; the rest are "news.")

§ The student interested in the varying voices of journalism might enjoy a related exercise. Take a paragraph or two from a number of different columns in your hometown newspaper, or take them from the mock newspaper that you just created yourself. Rewrite these passages in Newsweek-ese. What happens to the Events of the World when you do this?

1

All week long the Teletype machines connecting the low, concrete-block communications shack at the ranch with the White House chattered out draft sections of Lyndon Johnson's fifth annual assessment of the State of the Union—and revealed far more in the process about the state of the President. Gone were the personae of years past: Lyndon the keeper of the Kennedy flame, Lyndon the architect of his own Great Society, Lyndon the war President unwilling to cut back on the good works of peace. This week, so all the advance signals suggested, a new and unfamiliar LBJ would present himself to Congress and the nation on the eve of Presidential 1968. This New Lyndon, insiders said, would be austere, chary, cautious, long on sacrifice —and shorter on promises.

2

The first hurrah of the Democratic convention was still seven months off, but it was none too soon to start defusing the dual threat from without and within. And as the Democratic National Committee gathered for a final planning session at the site of the 1968 convention in Chicago last week, members soaked up some reassuring words of welcome from Mayor Richard J. Daley. "We won't let anyone come to Chicago and take over our city, our streets or our convention," Democrat Daley promised. "No man," he shouted, wagging a finger, "no thousands, will break up our convention."

That, of course, was precisely what militant comic Dick Gregory had lately threatened to do unless the city's ghetto conditions improved by convention time.

3

Diseased fish, higher auto prices, dental X-rays, tires—you name it, Ralph Nader was upset about it last week. As Everyman's self-appointed lobbyist in Washington, the lanky, sallow-faced lawyer raced through six eighteen-hour days, propelled by a fine sense of what his admirers call "controlled outrage" and his detractors describe as "fanaticism." From the time he arose at 7 A.M., until he tumbled back into bed long after midnight in his dingy $80-a-month furnished room, Nader was in perpetual motion—batting out prodding letters on his second-hand portable to the likes of Henry Ford II and Raymond C. Firestone, dashing to Congressional offices to supply tidbits of research in support of a consumer bill, keeping furtive rendezvous with Federal agency employees in downtown cafeterias, running up a $50 long-distance phone bill with calls to secret contacts in corporate offices and research laboratories.

4

Investors charged this way and that last week, churning up huge volume (65.9 million shares, highest weekly total on record) but showing no clear direction. Early in the week, blue-chip and cyclical issues were strong, and high flyers fell sharply. Then the conventional stocks faded—the Dow Jones industrial average finally closed at 898.98, for a 2-point loss—and many of the swingers came back into demand.

5

Last week the big freeze blew in from the Arctic—and the subzero temperatures and slashing winds kept most upper Midwestern folk close to their firesides and television sets. But out on the ice-locked lakes, like so many solitary seals, devout outdoorsmen were sitting patiently, hunkered over fishing lines. They were the ice anglers—a compleat breed Izaak Walton never dreamed of.

28

6

They come in almost as many styles as ladies' coifs—drooping Viva Zapatas, flaring Genghis Khans, bushy Karl Marxes and wispy Salvador Dalis. Whether they sweep or weep, mustaches are definitely staging a comeback, foliating the upper lips of American males ranging from pseudo-hippies to hip ad executives.

7

Normal Mailer's first film, *Wild 90*, dwells long and unlovingly on three guys from Brooklyn holed up in a loft-building hide-out. For 90 of the most uneventful minutes since Andy Warhol invented the creative coma, these boozily belligerent mugs fondle their firearms, trade scatological insult gags, and lay vague plans for a vague job they may pull if the spirit moves them, which it does not.

8

Washington thinks if you don't look at inflation it might go away.

Everyone in Washington over the age of 6 knows what inflation is, and how to stop it. But that would be politically painful, and if there is anything Washington can't stand, it's that!

So when unions demand inflationary (because unearned) wage increases, too many people stick their heads in the sand and refuse to see that that's the strongest inflationary pressure.

When corporations announce a modest increase in price (made necessary by wage increases) government screams in horror, and demands the increases be rescinded. So at that rate companies soon won't be able to afford the new machines which could hold costs and inflation down.

9

This year 100,000 people will die of kidney disease in this country.

A small city of men, women, and children is dying every year because kidney disease is something nice people don't talk about. Or know about. Or even care about. And yet we know how to save so many of them. With artificial kidney machines and kidney transplants. But there isn't enough money. A stupid thing like money.

10

It takes a bold man to say with certainty whether the market is going up or down. (Only your barber knows for sure.)

The market reacts not only to *news*, but to *rumors*. Rumors about a company's earnings, its management, its newest product.

Sometimes these rumors turn out to be true. More often they are false. True or false, they cause some people to buy and sell. The result is that prices move up or down—because the price of every stock depends on supply and demand.

Chapter 3

Reading a Novel

To catch the particular accent of the speaking voice in a piece
of writing is, as we have been noting, one of our primary
obligations as readers. Novels offer us a rich field for practice.
Sometimes, as in the first-person-singular narratives of Chapter
1, the voice in a novel can speak in the tones of the hero himself; he is the subject of the writing and he demands our
continuing attention. Other novels, of course, speak of their
heroes in the third person, as *other* people, people the narrator
knows about and tells us about. Occasionally a novel is written
in which varieties of voice inside a single volume can become
one of the reader's principal interests and delights. That is, the
author may present us, quite deliberately, with a whole parade
of personas, or perhaps it would be more accurate to say that
he presents us with a single brilliant persona capable of taking
on many roles in language. The very bravura of mixed styles
can be a major source of a reader's pleasure. Such is the novel
to be considered—in a very limited way—in this chapter: Saul
Bellow's *Herzog*, published in 1964.

It may seem heretical to suggest that this chapter can be
meaningful to the student without the necessity of his reading
the novel on which it is based. Yet in this case that is the fact.
By all means read the novel: it is a splendid one. But the par-

ticular limits of this discussion, and the exercise toward which it leads, can make sense to the student whether or not he is familiar with Bellow's book.

Herzog is the story of a professor of history in his forties who is having a rather bad time, principally because he has just suffered through his second divorce. In a series of not particularly rational events, Moses Herzog takes a train from his home, in New York City, to Martha's Vineyard, in Massachusetts, to see friends there, but returns immediately without even spending the night. Shortly thereafter, he goes to Chicago to see his daughter, and finds himself in an escapade with the police after a minor traffic accident. Extricated from these difficulties by a sympathetic brother, he returns east, this time to an old country house he owns in the Berkshires of western Massachusetts. Here we leave him about to be joined by his current mistress, and we sense at last that he is going to come out all right after all.

That doesn't sound like much of a plot, and it isn't. What is interesting about this book is the presentation of what goes on in Herzog's mind during these little adventures. Much of what goes on there is made evident to us through a series of letters he writes constantly throughout the book—letters he never sends. They are addressed to old and current girl friends, to people he knew in college, to relatives, to eminent people (Eisenhower, Stevenson), even to the "illustrious dead," including Nietzsche and Spinoza. It is these letters, with their variety of styles, that provide us with a whole picture gallery of personas, all in one book. For, like any educated and literate man, Herzog knows that when you address a letter to somebody, your style depends not only on what you want to say and the role you want to play, but also, and importantly, on whom you're talking to.

Here is the way the novel begins:

If I am out of my mind, it's all right with me, thought Moses Herzog.

Some people thought he was cracked and for a time he himself had doubted that he was all there.

In that first sentence we encounter the familiar situation of a narrator who is somehow "inside" the mind of his hero. Note that the narrator and hero are not identical, as they are in some first-person-singular fiction like *Huckleberry Finn* or *The Catcher in the Rye*. This is simply the report of a person who can quote for us what Herzog "thought." In the second sentence a more complicated relation between narrator and hero begins to emerge. "Some people thought he was cracked . . ." Is this the narrator's statement, from his own knowledge, or is it a kind of indirect echo of something Herzog is thinking, such as "Some people think I'm cracked"? This last possibility seems supported by the remainder of the sentence, which reports again on the thought processes of Herzog—"he himself doubted." Furthermore the sense we may have that Herzog is almost being quoted throughout may be caused by the colloquial expressions—"cracked" and "all there."

In sum, we have a narrator's voice here that is apparently very close to the sound of Herzog's own voice, even though the story is told in the third person. Occasionally, as the book proceeds, the narrator slides unobtrusively from third to first person, and we hardly feel the change. That is, the narrator can move from his own language into direct quotation of his hero, and back again, and we scarcely know the difference.

But the particular interest we have in this book as students of style is not so much the subtle interrelationship of narrator and hero, fascinating though that is. More to the point for our purposes here are the choices of style made by Herzog himself in his somewhat "cracked" efforts to come to terms with his mixed-up life and his mixed-up world. During the novel, as we have said, Herzog is beset by the curious compulsion to write letters to people, and these letters begin to fill up a notebook he carries with him wherever he goes. From the novelist's point of view, such a device offers a perfect opportunity for that "bravura" performance of mixed styles we earlier referred to. It is also a device, of course, for getting "on paper" a version of Herzog's thinking processes.

Perhaps the variety of Herzog's voices as he addresses these fictional letters to one "recipient" after another can remind us of the facility and flexibility that an educated individual in our society might ideally possess. Herzog writes foolish things sometimes, but his trouble is not lack of stylistic flexibility in response to different situations and audiences. Sometimes, writing an old friend, he can be abrupt and colloquial:

What's gotten into you? I often read "human-interest" paragraphs but I never expect them to be about my friends. You can imagine how it shook me to see your name in the Post. *Have you gone crazy? I know you adored that monkey of yours, and I'm sorry he's dead. But you should have known better than to try to revive him by mouth-to-mouth respiration. Especially as Rocco died of TB and must have been jumping with bugs.*

A few pages later he can glide easily into the appropriate mode for writing a business concern, though this time, after a couple of sentences, he "forgets himself" and lapses into a more personal tone:

Credit Department, Marshall Field & Co. I am no longer responsible for the debts of Madeline P. Herzog. As of March 10, we ceased to be husband and wife. So don't send me any more bills—I was knocked over by the last—more than four hundred dollars. For purchases made after the separation.

He can immediately follow this with a letter to a scientific author whose work he has recently read:

Dear Professor Hoyle, I don't think I understand just how the Gold-Pore Theory works. How the heavier metals—iron, nickel—get to the center of the earth, I think I see. But what about the concentration of lighter metals? Also, in your explanation of the formation of smaller planets, including our tragic earth, *you speak of adhesive materials that bind the agglomerates of precipitated matter.*

A few pages later, in a high heat of moral indignation, he begins a letter to a distant acquaintance, then crosses it out and instead decides to make the point by writing *The New York Times.* See how his styles shift accordingly:

Mr. Emmett Strawforth, U.S. Public Health Service, he wrote. *Dear Emmett, I saw you on television making a damn fool of yourself. Since we were undergraduates together (M. E. Herzog '38) I feel free to tell you what I think of your philosophy.*
Herzog crossed this out and readdressed his letter to the *New York Times. Again a government scientist, Dr. Emmett Strawforth, has come forward with the Philosophy of Risk in the controversy over fallout, to which has now been added the problem of chemical pesti-*

*cides, contamination of ground water, etc. I am as deeply concerned
with the social and ethical reasoning of scientists as I am with those
other forms of poisoning.*

Throughout the novel, Bellow uses the typographical device of
italics to distinguish the letters Herzog writes from the rest of the
narrative. This means that we can recognize, sometimes inside
individual sentences, those expressions that are addressed to a
recipient, via a letter, and other expressions not so addressed.
The shifts are accompanied by changes of voice. In the letter to
Professor Hoyle, just quoted, Herzog writes:

Also, in your explanation of the formation of smaller planets, including our tragic earth, *you speak of adhesive materials* . . .

Here the reference to our own earth as "tragic" is a side comment
that Herzog makes to himself, not to Professor Hoyle. Why? Because in writing to a scientist on a scientific matter, one does not
conventionally indulge in such an emotional adjective. This
would not conform to the persona appropriate for the circumstances. Yet it is a measure of Herzog's own sanity (cracked or
not) that *he* can use both kinds of language, practically simultaneously, and distinguish between them. He is not so innocent
as to believe that a complicated state of mind can be finally
expressed in one voice, even though he also knows that in the
"practical" situation of writing a letter, especially to someone he
does not know intimately, it is conventional to adopt one kind of
style and stick to it.

On the other hand, since these letters are not going to be sent
to anyone, as Herzog well knows while he writes them, he sometimes does indulge himself a little, lets his voice change in ways
that are in fact unconventional, as he did in his letter to Marshall
Field & Co.

Dear Governor Stevenson, Herzog wrote, gripping his seat in the
hurtling train. *Just a word with you, friend. I supported you in 1952.
Like many others I thought this country might be ready for its great
age in the world* . . .

Here, because Herzog is writing a letter that is not a letter, he
can buttonhole Stevenson in a manner that would be unthinkable

in real life or a real letter. (Stevenson was of course still alive when this book was published.) *"Just a word with you, friend."* Perhaps this expression contributes to our understanding of Herzog's emotional state, his highly personal *caring* about what he is writing. Often one may be desperately and personally involved in an issue as one writes a letter to a public official about it, but one's expression must conform to styles that maintain considerable social distance. Herzog (or Bellow) has invented a form, the fictional letter, that avoids these difficulties, and permits a play between direct informal address (*"Just a word with you"*) and the more formal kind of language appropriate to such documents (*"Like many others I thought . . ."*).

Here are some further passages from Herzog's letters that will display his versatility, especially as we see him confronting some serious and public concerns. Writing to the long-dead philosopher Friedrich Nietzsche, he begins a little frivolously, and he never loses a direct approach to his "reader," but the issues and much of the language are solemn and academic:

Dear Herr Nietzsche—My dear sir, May I ask a question from the floor? You speak of the power of the Dionysian spirit to endure the sight of the Terrible, the Questionable, to allow itself the luxury of Destruction, to witness Decomposition, Hideousness, Evil. All this the Dionysian spirit can do because it has the same power of recovery as Nature itself. Some of these expressions, I must tell you, have a very Germanic ring. A phrase like the "luxury of Destruction" is positively Wagnerian, and I know how you came to despise all that sickly Wagnerian idiocy and bombast. Now we've seen enough destruction to test the power of the Dionysian spirit amply, and where are the heroes who have recovered from it?

Here he discusses suffering (with his own suffering much in mind), and the language turns religious:

You have to have the power to employ pain, to repent, to be illuminated, you must have the opportunity and even the time. With the religious, the love of suffering is a form of gratitude to experience or an opportunity to experience evil and change it into good. They believe the spiritual cycle can and will be completed in a man's existence and he will somehow make use of his suffering, if only in the last moments of his life, when the mercy of God will reward him with a vision of the truth, and he will die transfigured. But this is a special exercise. More commonly suffering breaks people, crushes them, and is simply unilluminating. You see how gruesomely human beings are destroyed by pain, when they have the added torment of losing their humanity first, so that their death is a total defeat, and then you write about "modern forms of Orphism" and about "people who are not afraid of suffering" and throw in other such cocktail-party expressions. Why not say rather that people of powerful imagination, given to dreaming deeply and to raising up marvelous and self-sufficient fictions, turn to suffering sometimes to cut into their bliss, as people pinch themselves to feel awake.

Or here, poetic and passionate, he writes in the spasmodic sentences that characterize still another of his styles:

The dream of man's heart, however much we may distrust and resent it, is that life may complete itself in significant patterns. Some incomprehensible way. Before death. Not irrationally but incomprehensibly fulfilled. Spared by these clumsy police guardians, you get one last chance to know justice. Truth.

Herzog's various self-conscious styles in his letters have their counterpart in his self-consciousness generally. He is forever examining himself, appraising, usually ruefully. There is much to make fun of in his own predicament, as he is himself painfully aware. He arrives at Martha's Vineyard, on that abortive trip to visit friends, and is oddly able to stand aside from himself, sizing himself up. It is as if he were taking on still another role, quite outside of himself, as a spectator.

And what a look he had—such a face! Just then his state of being was so curious that he was compelled, himself, to see it—eager, grieving, fantastic, dangerous, crazed and, to the point of death, "comical."

This habit of wry self-appraisal seems appropriate to a man who in his writing can take on such varied voices. When Herzog indulges in self-criticism, he seems amused at the very clichés of his self-attack, while at the same time he cringes from his own body blows. He lashes out at himself: *"Losing self-respect! Lacking clear ideas!"* But such phrases seem to come from the most simple-minded of evangelical tirades. On another occasion he ticks himself off as "an eager, hasty, self-intense, and comical person." "Poor fellow, his health was not good," he says of himself, and in the very next sentence: "Herzog was grinning as he thought of the pills he had taken, and the milk he had drunk in the night." Is he sorry for himself or laughing at himself? Herzog's intense awareness of his own inner muddle is summed up in a phrase he applies to himself early in the novel—*"that suffering joker."* The joker who suffers, and who knows that he jokes as he suffers, is the man equipped with exactly that degree of awareness necessary to adopt dozens of roles as letter-writer.

And even as Herzog suffers, his suffering is considerably undercut by his circumstances, which are sometimes downright enviable. He is neither cold nor hungry; he never lacks for women; his very play with his own tribulations on paper suggests that he is far from true despair. All this too he knows, as he abruptly addresses himself in that omnipresent notebook:

> *Moses!* he wrote, *winning as he weeps, weeping as he wins. Evidently can't believe in victories.*
> *Hitch your agony to a star.*

Here the reader must of course recognize the allusion to the tag from Emerson ("Hitch your wagon to a star"). But equally important, he must sense the sort of personality implied by the language. This is a voice capable of uttering a ludicrous pun in the midst of self-analysis and self-pity. Here is a character who can turn on his own suffering and make it into sudden foolishness.

In Herzog's simultaneous awareness of his own suffering and his own foolishness, there may be a difficulty that is worth pausing over, for it is a difficulty familiar to many modern novels. As we read all those letters never posted, we may be torn between two conflicting attitudes. "What a sure understanding of the situation and audience!" "What a crazy thing that is, to write all that stuff and never even buy a stamp!" Which attitude does the persona of the novel invite, which does the ideal reader adopt? Both, probably, from time to time, and sometimes both at once. We have few sure indications whether to consider Herzog primarily as a pitiable sufferer or primarily as an outrageous clown. Why this confusion? Precisely because, as we noted earlier, the narrator of this book is so close to the hero that he never backs off to tell us *what* to think. We simply have to deal with the contradictory evidence before us as best we can. Some modern critics, notably Wayne Booth in *The Rhetoric of Fiction*, have protested that this way of writing is an evasion of an author's responsibility to state an attitude and set the reader right. Whatever your judgment in this argument may be, the fact is that a do-it-yourself implication is discoverable in much of modern art, and we face more ambiguity of attitude than readers have tolerated in the past. But let no one suppose that this ambiguity is infinite, at least in *Herzog*. It is *not* true that one reader's response is just as appropriate as any other's, or that anything goes. For example, a bad reader might interpret this novel entirely as the pathetic story of a heroic individual caught in the stresses of complex modern life. True, but not enough. Another bad reader might dismiss *Herzog* as funny—no more and no less. Between these misreadings of voice, these regrettable extremes, there is an area where good readers may properly agree to disagree.

When Herzog says of himself, "Losing self-respect! Lacking clear ideas!"—do we laugh at him, for the deficiencies named and for his corny way of expressing them? Or do we laugh with him, for his ironic sense of his own clichés? These are hard questions to answer, but at least we can say this: not to laugh at all is to be a bad reader, unaware of voice. Herzog himself can express his own difficulties in a far different style, as he does in a letter to a Monsignor Hilton:

> But I, a learned specialist in intellectual history, handicapped by emotional confusion . . . Resisting the argument that scientific thought has put into disorder all considerations based on value . . . Convinced that the extent of universal space does not destroy human value, that the realm of facts and that of values are not eternally separated.

Note here the formal tone, but note also the incomplete sentences.

It is precisely this achievement of living comfortably with ambiguity that becomes a major victory of Moses Herzog in the novel. "*Allow me modestly to claim*," he writes near the end of the book, "*that I am much better now at ambiguities*," though he goes on to attack the fashionable intellectual ambiguity that questions the values of civilization itself. On the last pages there occurs a dialogue with himself that may seem, from a suffering joker, a little too pat:

"But what do you want, Herzog?" "But that's just it—not a solitary thing. I am pretty well satisfied to be, to be just as it is willed, and for as long as I may remain in occupancy."

A possible exercise for the student writer in response to this chapter can be the obvious one: write some letters. Write paragraphs to your congressman, your milkman, your broker. Write to the new girlfriend you are courting, and the old one you are breaking up with. (What is the rhetoric of a "Dear John" letter?) Write to *Life*, to *Playboy*. Write a grateful note to your roommate after spending a weekend at his home, and another grateful note to his mother. Would you be willing to send these letters, given the circumstances? Why or why not?

§ Now here is another exercise in style. Write a fictional letter (one you could not conceivably send) and use Bellow's device of italics to distinguish between the language appropriate for the recipient and the language that is not. For example, a formal letter of protest to a draft board, a police chief, or a dean could be peppered and punctuated with phrases of a very different style, nonitalicized. Invective, personal attacks, cries of passion or alarm, private reminiscence—have a good time. Be a conventional persona, and "be yourself," simultaneously.

§ Still another kind of exercise, in reading more than in writing, can be based on close examinations of the opening paragraphs of various novels, novels that do not speak to us in the first person. Who is the narrator that addresses us? What is his relation to his hero, or to the character he is bringing on stage? Are we to presume that the narrator's language echoes the way the character might express himself, as in *Herzog*? Or does the character, or hero, inhabit an entirely different linguistic world from that of the narrator?

Here is a mixed bag of openings of novels, and of one short story, for your consideration. In each of them a narrator is bringing onstage a hero or other character for your pleasure. What are the relations between these people?

1

Mrs. Dalloway said she would buy the flowers herself.

For Lucy had her work cut out for her. The doors would be taken off their hinges; Rumpelmayer's men were coming. And then, thought Clarissa Dalloway, what a morning—fresh as if issued to children on a beach.

What a lark! What a plunge! For so it had always seemed to her, when, with a little squeak of the hinges, which she could hear now, she had burst open the French windows and plunged at Bourton into the open air. How fresh, how calm, stiller than this of course, the air was in the early morning; like the flap of a wave; the kiss of a wave; chill and sharp and yet (for a girl of eighteen as she then was) solemn, feeling as she did, standing there at the open window, that something awful was about to happen; looking at the flowers, at the trees with the smoke winding off them and the rooks rising, falling; standing and looking until Peter Walsh said, "Musing among the vegetables?"—was that it?—"I prefer men to cauliflowers"—was that it? He must have said it at breakfast one morning when she had gone out on to the terrace—Peter Walsh. He would be back from India one of these days, June or July, she forgot which, for his letters were awfully dull; it was his sayings one remembered; his eyes, his pocket-knife, his smile, his grumpiness and, when millions of things had utterly vanished—how strange it was!—a few sayings like this about cabbages.

2

The store in which the Justice of the Peace's court was sitting smelled of cheese. The boy, crouched on his nail keg at the back of the crowded room, knew he smelled cheese, and more: from where he sat he could see the ranked shelves close-packed with the solid, squat, dynamic shapes of tin cans whose labels his stomach read, not from the lettering which meant nothing to his mind but from the scarlet devils and the silver curve of fish—this, the cheese which he knew he smelled and the hermetic meat which his intestines believed he smelled coming in intermittent gusts momentary and brief between the other constant one, the smell and sense just a little of fear because mostly of despair and grief, the old fierce pull of blood. He could not see the table where the Justice sat and before which his father and his father's enemy (*our enemy* he thought in that despair; *ourn! mine and hisn both! He's my father!*) stood, but he could hear them, the two of them that is, because his father had said no word yet:

"But what proof have you, Mr. Harris?"

3

It was admitted by all her friends, and also by her enemies,—who were in truth the more numerous and active body of the two, that Lizzie Greystock had done very well with herself. We will tell the story of Lizzie Greystock from the beginning, but we will not dwell over it at great length, as we might do if we loved her. She was the only child of old Admiral Greystock, who in the latter years of his life was much perplexed by the possession of a daughter. The admiral was a man who liked whist, wine,—and wickedness in general we may perhaps say, and whose ambition it was to live every day of his life up to the end of it. People say that he succeeded, and that the whist, wine, and wickedness were there, at the side even of his dying bed. He had no particular fortune, and yet his daughter, when she was little more than a child, went about everywhere with jewels on her fingers, and red gems hanging round her neck, and yellow gems pendent from her ears, and white gems shining in her black hair. She was hardly nineteen when her father died and she was taken home by that dreadful old termagant, her aunt Lady Linlithgow. Lizzie would have sooner gone to any other friend or relative, had there been any other friend or relative to take her possessed of a house in town.

4

Stately, plump Buck Mulligan came from the stairhead, bearing a bowl of lather on which a mirror and a razor lay crossed. A yellow dressinggown, ungirdled, was sustained gently behind him by the mild morning air. He held the bowl aloft and intoned:
—*Introibo ad altare Dei.*
Halted, he peered down the dark winding stairs and called up coarsely:
—Come up, Kinch. Come up, you fearful jesuit.
Solemnly he came forward and mounted the round gunrest. He faced about and blessed gravely thrice the tower, the surrounding country and the awaking mountains. Then, catching sight of Stephen Dedalus, he bent towards him and made rapid crosses in the air, gurgling in his throat and shaking his head. Stephen Dedalus, displeased and sleepy, leaned his arms on the top of the staircase and looked coldly at the shaking gurgling face that blessed him, equine in its length, and at the light untonsured hair, grained and hued like pale oak.

5

When Caroline Meeber boarded the afternoon train for Chicago, her total outfit consisted of a small trunk, a cheap imitation alligator-skin satchel, a small lunch in a paper box, and a yellow leather snap purse, containing her ticket, a scrap of paper with her sister's address in Van Buren Street, and four dollars in money. It was August, 1889. She was eighteen years of age, bright, timid, and full of the illusions of ignorance and youth. Whatever touch of regret at parting characterised her thoughts, it was certainly not for advantages now being given up. A gush of tears at her mother's farewell kiss, a touch in her throat when the cars clacked by the flour mill where her father worked by the day, a pathetic sigh as the familiar green environs of the village passed in review, and the threads which bound her so lightly to girlhood and home were irretrievably broken.

6

"You won't be late?" There was anxiety in Marjorie Carling's voice, there was something like entreaty.

"No, I won't be late," said Walter, unhappily and guiltily certain that he would be. Her voice annoyed him. It drawled a little, it was too refined—even in misery.

"Not later than midnight." She might have reminded him of the time when he never went out in the evenings without her. She might have done so; but she wouldn't; it was against her principles; she didn't want to force his love in any way.

"Well, call it one. You know what these parties are." But as a matter of fact, she didn't know, for the good reason that, not being his wife, she wasn't invited to them. She had left her husband to live with Walter Bidlake; and Carling, who had Christian scruples, was feebly a sadist and wanted to take his revenge, refused to divorce her. It was two years now, since they had begun to live together. Only two years; and now, already, he had ceased to love her, he had begun to love someone else. The sin was losing its only excuse, the social discomfort its sole palliation. And she was with child.

7

Miss Brooke had that kind of beauty which seems to be thrown into relief by poor dress. Her hand and wrist were so finely formed that she could wear sleeves not less bare of style than those in which the Blessed Virgin appeared to Italian painters; and her profile as well as her stature and bearing seemed to gain the more dignity from her plain garments, which by the side of provincial fashion gave her the impressiveness of a fine quotation from the Bible—or from one of our elder poets—in a paragraph of to-day's newspaper. She was usually spoken of as being remarkably clever, but with the addition that her sister Celia had more common-sense. Nevertheless, Celia wore scarcely more trimmings; and it was only to close observers that her dress differed from her sister's, and had a shade of coquetry in its arrangements; for Miss Brooke's plain dressing was due to mixed conditions, in most of which her sister shared. The pride of being ladies had something to do with it: the Brooke connections, though not exactly aristocratic, were unquestionably "good": if you inquired backward for a generation or two, you would not find any yard-measuring or parcel-tying forefathers,—anything lower than an admiral or a clergyman; and there was even an ancestor discernible as a Puritan gentleman who served under Cromwell, but afterwards conformed, and managed to come out of all political troubles as the proprietor of a respectable family estate. Young women of such birth, living in a quiet country-house, and attending a village church hardly larger than a parlour, naturally regarded frippery as the ambition of a huckster's daughter.

8

The mirror reflected what seemed at first a priest. A white robe, which fell from his thick shoulders in crescent folds, circumscribed with diminishing accuracy the ponderous art of his great head, and gave to his obesity the suggestion of vulnerability rather than strength as he sat face to face with the fact of himself. This effect was intensified by the resignation with which he suffered what might have been his acolyte, also dressed in white, either to anoint his flourishing, gray-brown hair as if in preparation for some imminent solemnity or to give it a tonsure. The precise nature of the operation was of apparently little concern to him, however, for he fixed his eyes simply upon the mirror, which reflected not so much any details of activity as certain implications of priestliness. The activity, the ritual failed to attract his attention because he regarded instead only the image of himself, of Tristram Bone, removed from circumstance, with a look of profound intensity in which there was, nevertheless, no curiosity; a look he had seen occasionally pass between lovers, possible only after a long romance.

9

The grandmother didn't want to go to Florida. She wanted to visit some of her connections in east Tennessee and she was seizing at every chance to change Bailey's mind. Bailey was the son she lived with, her only boy. He was sitting on the edge of his chair at the table, bent over the orange sports section of the *Journal*. "Now look here, Bailey," she said, "see here, read this," and she stood with one hand on her thin hip and the other rattling the newspaper at his bald head. "Here this fellow that calls himself The Misfit is aloose from the Federal Pen and headed toward Florida and you read here what it says he did to those people. Just you read it. I wouldn't take my children in any direction with a criminal like that aloose in it. I couldn't answer to my conscience if I did."

45

10

A man came down the steps cut in the rock. By nature agile, he made the descent with unusual caution, placing each foot first tentatively then extra firmly. He did well to—the steps, inexpertly hewn at some unknown time, were no two alike, and were this evening slippery after rain; moreover, he carried, balanced against his midriff, a lidless white cardboard box toppling with a miscellany of objects.

Part II

WRITING
The Voices We Pitch

Chapter 4

Writing for Tone

Imagine yourself at your desk, preparing to do an assignment. What is it like, sitting there at that desk? Try talking to yourself about what it is like:

> I am sitting here at this desk. The green blotter is torn at the edges. I'm not sure how to do this assignment. This chair is hard and uncomfortable. I hope tonight's supper is better than last night. I wonder why Jane didn't write today. I think I will put my feet up and try leaning back.

This random list of thoughts and sensations is not very interesting. Why? One reason is that the speaker is talking to himself: there is no address to someone else, no acknowledgment of another human being. Let's play Herzog again and make another try, in the form of a letter:

> Dear Jane: I've been sitting here at this desk for fifteen minutes, trying to get started on a history assignment, but actually I've mostly been thinking about you. There's probably some good reason why you didn't write today, and then I have to admit I didn't write either. I look at my books and things on this desk and hardly see them—on the green blotter there's a scrawl that I think says "Dear Jane" backwards.

49

Now let's try a version that generalizes and addresses a wide public audience. One way to do this is by changing the word "I" into an abstraction like "the American student."

The American student, seated at his desk with his daily assignment, is a bemused creature, easily distracted, far from intellectual. Ill prepared to confront the demands his education makes of him, he is likely to find refuge in dawdling and day-dreaming.

Or, to take another line:

All over America, as day darkens into evening, young men and women in hundreds of colleges bend over their appointed tasks, their minds constantly expanding as they undergo what we call the educational process.

The kind of audience this sentence is aimed at is somewhat different from the one we have just addressed. The assumed reader now is someone who is unoffended by certain phrases that, for others, will seem pompous and overused. "As day darkens into evening." "Bend over their appointed tasks." How do you react to a persona who seriously employs such phrases? Or—and this is difficult to tell without a larger context—can you see the persona as a gentle mocker, making fun of such language as he uses it?

Now put yourself in time; make a little history.

When millions of young Americans are seated at millions of desks in hundreds of colleges all over America, the contrast with the recent past is striking. Where only a tiny fraction of the population aspired to higher education a generation or two ago, now it is almost demanded that every 18-year-old has the right to a place on a campus.

Now let's theorize—what might happen or could happen?

It is the millions of individual students now at their desks who are bound to make profound alterations in our political patterns. In another generation or two, our leaders will simply have to begin talking sense to the electorate, for the electorate will be gullible no longer.

You have come a distance, from an idler at your desk to a hopeful sign of the political future. You have manipulated your "self" so as to make yourself significant in various ways. But more than that, you have changed your voice, the voice that you took on as you talked or wrote in this way or that way. You kept changing your persona, and in doing so you invited the attention of a wide range of assumed readers.

All writing, all expression, as we have been repeatedly pointing out, implies a self-definition, and flexibility in such self-defining is a desirable quality—at least in the view of this book. The larger one's repertoire of selves, the more wisely one can choose an effective voice in a given situation. But we ought to concede a possible danger in this position. Perhaps you know someone who is a natural ham, who imitates others constantly, playacts incessantly, and manifests an astonishing variety of selves. But he never seems to say anything! Such people certainly exist, but they are rare, and they do not need the argument of this book. For most of us, our problem is just the other way: we are limited to a relatively small selection of voices, and our characteristic style is all too omnipresent and inflexible. For most people, a wider, not a narrower, range of roles is worth seeking to improve relations with others.

But granting that, granting the importance of a whole battery of available personas, how does one choose a particular persona at a given moment? Mere whim, impulse, inspiration, self-indulgence? Sometimes, no doubt, these will do, and no one should write them off as inconsequential. But obviously, our decision about who to be as we address ourselves to a task in communication is a *controlled* decision. It is controlled by strong forces *in the situation*, two of which we have already encountered many times in this book. One is *audience*—the reader, listener. We create different personas for ourselves depending on the individual or crowd we are addressing, as in the composing of those Herzogian letters at the end of the previous chapter. Vocabulary, sentence structure, style, vary depending on whether it's an article for students of history or a letter to Jane. The second great controlling factor is our *subject,* our argument, our purpose, the point we are trying to make. We create a different persona for ourselves depending on whether we're speaking of sunsets or sociology, cabbages or kings. And the values we put upon these things, our feelings for or against them, have a further bearing on the voices we choose.

51

There are, then, these three ways of discussing how we control the words we choose: the voice or persona, the audience, the subject or argument. Everybody knows this, everybody "controls himself" somewhat, according to these considerations. To a degree, every sane person from the age of four changes himself and his language in response to audience and subject. The purpose of this book is to make that degree a little larger and more conscious, so that we may widen our range of possibilities and make our way in the world with greater power, greater sympathy for others, and more fun.

Will a diagram help?

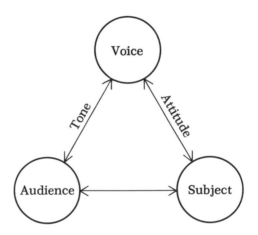

It may be reassuring to know that the three labels we are using here—voice, audience, subject—approximate the terms of a famous triad proposed over two thousand years ago by Aristotle, in a treatise called *Rhetoric*. But we are not so much concerned with the venerable prestige of these terms as we are with their usefulness for us here and now. In this chapter we will be attempting to describe relations between the first two, voice and audience, the relation we call *tone*. In Chapter 5, we will turn to relations of voice and subject, or *attitude*. But throughout, as you will quickly see, we will not be able to discuss these relations in isolation; all three of our terms are involved in a constantly shifting interaction. When we change our voice, we inevitably shift our judgment of what we are talking about and we alter our expression of fellow-feeling toward our listener. If we find ourselves facing a different audience, we alter our own mask (if we are alert), and we probably cannot help altering our attitude toward our subject as we do so. If we "change the subject," as we say, altogether—from kings to cabbages for instance—our actual audience may remain the same, but the way we treat that audience is likely to shift as we move from king-language to cabbage-language. For the writer or speaker sensitive to his situation, a difference in any one aspect of the communication will force differences in other aspects as well.

Suppose we begin illustrating some of these interconnections by recalling our discussion of first-person-singular narratives in Chapter 1. You will remember the crude, general distinctions we made there between writer-style and talker-style, or, more familiarly, between formal and informal uses of language. We observed how a traditional sort of speaker, however witty and urbane (like David Copperfield), tends to keep his reader at some *distance*, while the sort of colloquial narrator we encountered in Holden Caulfield approaches the reader more *closely*, sharing his experience more intimately. The metaphor we are using in this explanation is the metaphor of physical space. Much of our discussion of tone can be carried on with the assistance of this metaphor. Ask the question: How close is the imagined speaker to the imagined listener? Is the speaker talking to the listener as they sit face to face, or side by side? Or is the speaker, as it were, reading to the listener, perhaps from a platform? Answers to such questions will help us make distinctions of tone.

Let us now recall the sound of the two voices we have just referred to, and this time we might let them run on a little more than we permitted ourselves in Chapter 1.

DAVID COPPERFIELD

Whether I shall turn out to be the hero of my own life, or whether that station will be held by anybody else, these pages must show. To begin my life with the beginning of my life, I record that I was born (as I have been informed and believe) on a Friday, at twelve o'clock at night. It was remarked that the clock began to strike, and I began to cry, simultaneously.

In consideration of the day and hour of my birth, it was declared by the nurse and by some sage women in the neighborhood who had taken a lively interest in me several months before there was any possibility of our becoming personally acquainted, first that I was destined to be unlucky in life; and secondly, that I was privileged to see ghosts and spirits: both these gifts inevitably attaching, as they believed, to all unlucky infants of either gender born towards the small hours on a Friday night.

HOLDEN CAULFIELD

If you really want to hear about it, the first thing you'll probably want to know is where I was born, and what my lousy childhood was like, and how my parents were occupied and all before they had me, and all that David Copperfield kind of crap, but I don't feel like going into it, if you want to know the truth. In the first place, that stuff bores me, and in the second place, my parents would have about two hemorrhages apiece if I told anything pretty personal about them. They're quite touchy about anything like that, especially my father. They're *nice* and all—I'm not saying that—but they're also touchy as hell. Besides, I'm not going to tell you my whole goddam autobiography or anything. I'll just tell you about this madman stuff that happened to me around last Christmas just before I got pretty run-down and had to come out here and take it easy.

Suppose you were about to write an account of your own life. How would you begin? What about the circumstances of your birth and early life? Before going further, compose on the spot a couple of hundred words which might serve as an opening or self-introduction to your own autobiography.

And when you have done that, let us return to Messrs. Copperfield and Caulfield to look a little more carefully at the way their voices were created. This is to recapitulate, in somewhat greater detail, some distinctions we made in Chapter 1.

What are some observations we can make about Copperfield's uses of words that make him as a character distinct from Caulfield? Look once more at that opening sentence. "Whether I . . . or whether I . . . , these pages must show." We have two fairly elaborate subordinate clauses, and then, finally, at the very end of the sentence, comes the main subject-verb pattern. A sentence organized in this way is called a *periodic* sentence; it forces us to wait, in a kind of suspense, before we learn what the sentence is saying. It is of course a technique far more characteristic of writer-style than of talker-style. People simply do not speak casually to one another in periodic sentences; instead, they state their case immediately (subject-verb), qualifying it afterward with modifying phrases and clauses. That last sentence is a good example, and so is the one you are reading right now. Such sentences are called *loose*. Almost all the sentences we read and write, speak and hear, are in fact loose, so that when we do encounter a true periodic sentence, like Copperfield's, we recognize that we are meeting a relatively formal, literary voice. In spite of the voice's geniality (in this case), he keeps us at a fair distance. You will recall our revision of that sentence in Chapter 1, in which we brought the reader closer to the speaker by using talker-style. One of the changes we made, we can now observe, was from a periodic to a loose sentence structure.

I don't know whether I'll be the hero of this story or not—maybe somebody else will.

Caulfield's sentences are uniformly loose, as the first sentence, with its trailing appendages, should illustrate.

Another stylistic feature of that first sentence of Copperfield's is one we have pointed to before. It is what we call *parallel structure*. "Whether I . . . or whether I . . ." These clauses are so phrased that they are balanced, one against the other, with repeated wording to signal the parallelism. Again, this is an effect more familiar in writer-style, for it gives an impression of having been thought out in advance, consciously constructed, in a way that most talk cannot be. Here are some other such balances in Copperfield.

"the clock began to strike, and I began to cry"; "first that I was destined . . . and secondly, that I was privileged."

There is parallelism in Caulfield's language too, but quite different in structure and effect: "In the first place . . . and in the second place . . ." But count the number of words appearing after each of those signaling phrases. "In the first place," then four words, "in the second place," then fifteen words. The two are precisely unbalanced, as befits our teenage speaker. The difference can be appreciated if we rewrite to make the two parts closer in wording and more equal in length. "In the first place, that stuff bores me, and in the second place, that stuff pleases me." Meaning aside, this is much too neat a sentence structure for the likes of Holden.

Another observation we ought to make about Copperfield's language, as opposed to Caulfield's, has to do with a single part of speech—his verbs. What is noteworthy about Copperfield's verbs? A singularly high proportion of them are in the *passive voice:* "will be held," "it was remarked," "I was destined," and so on. (We are using the word voice now in the strictly grammatical sense—active and passive voice of a verb. Be sure you understand the difference between this sense and the rhetorical meaning of voice as used throughout this book.) Some teachers advise students never to use the passive voice under any circumstances, but that of course is overdoing it. The problem is to understand what passive voice does to the tone and to the whole communication. "It was declared by some sage women . . ." What happens if we attempt a revision into active voice: "Some sage women declared . . ."? The focus, in the original, is on the remark, not on the women. More than that, the speaker suggests some distance on his part from the whole scene. He expresses detachment. Repeated use of the passive voice will create a speaker who is remote from his subject, dispassionate, and this in turn produces the effect of a speaker distant from his reader as well.

It should be added, though, that in Copperfield the repeated passives and other formal devices produce a kind of exaggeration that is finally humorous. It is as if he were saying, "Observe with what absurd elegance I discourse on my innocent babyhood and those silly 'sage women.'" We have spoken of Copperfield's "geniality"; certainly we do not take these balances and passives and lengthy clauses with the solemnity that is so suffocating when such devices are found in textbooks, committee reports, and political speeches.

Passive voice is much less frequent in Caulfield's language, though it is not totally absent ("was born," "were occupied"). Instead, Caulfield uses some devices of talker-style calculated to bring the reader in close. Recall our metaphor of physical space. In Chapter 1 we noted two devices Caulfield uses to evoke the talker's relation. One is his direct appeal to us via the second person pronoun ("If you really want to hear about it"); you will observe no appearance of the word *you* in Copperfield. Another is the use of contractions ("you'll," "don't"), which are of course an obvious method of echoing the sound of talk.

We have then a very short list of observations we have made about the styles of these two passages—observations that begin to explain how it is that Caulfield seems intent on being close to us, in his tone, while Copperfield keeps his distance. Here is our list:

COPPERFIELD	CAULFIELD
a periodic sentence	loose sentences
considerable parallel structure	little parallel structure
several verbs in passive voice	almost all verbs active
no second person pronoun	direct reference to the reader "you"
no contractions	contractions

Put baldly, the characteristics of style in the left-hand column work to create distance between speaker and reader, whereas those on the right tend to bring speaker and reader closer together. Naturally, this is only the beginning of a list you could make for yourself, a list ten times as long as this.

Now suppose we return to your own autobiographical fragment, the one you composed in response to that directive paragraph a few pages back. What about your voice and tone in that fragment? Were you removed from your reader, or close to him? Does reference to the lists above help you to decide which you were?

In any event, your next step is to do some rewriting of your own. Take your little opening passage, and try changing voices— twice. In your first revision, into writer-style, keep your distance from your reader by any changes in wording and organization that seem appropriate. At least five things you can do are: include a periodic sentence, and a couple of samples of neat parallel structure; put several verbs in the passive voice; avoid the second person pronoun; and use no contractions. You will probably want to change vocabulary to some extent too, but these revisions of grammar and arrangement may do much of your work for you. In your second rewriting, work just the other way in order to bring your reader close—to where you share your experience intimately with him. Make your sentences loose, avoid parallel structure, keep your verbs in the active voice, address the reader with *you*, and include a few contractions. You may find yourself preferring one or the other of these revisions to your original effort. If so, you may have discovered in the process a persona more attractive to you for this purpose.

Notice how, when you undertake an operation like this, your presumed audience seems to change. In your first revision you might be addressing, say, a college admissions officer; in the second you are addressing a friend, probably of your own age, with whom you are on easygoing terms.

In the practical process of writing, of choosing an appropriate tone, our problem is of course rarely this easy. That is, we are seldom faced with a crude choice between "writer-style" and "talker-style"—what we have to do instead is pick out some particular relation with our reader along a whole graduated scale of possibilities, from remotest distance to closest friendship. Even in a simple operation such as stating the place and date of one's birth, these problems of choice arise.

Place of birth: Jacksonville, Fla.
Date: Jan. 19, 1950
    The utter impersonality of a driver's license or job application.

The writer was born in Jacksonville, Florida, 19 January 1950.
    Flat and impersonal, but at least the politeness of full sentence structure and no abbreviations.

I was born in Jacksonville, Florida, on the 19th of January, 1950.
    Here enters a personal pronoun, and the date is rephrased more conversationally.

I was born in Jacksonville in January, 1950.
    Persona now assumes the reader knows what state Jacksonville is in, and of course this implies some degree of closeness between them. The date is accordingly less precise.

Where was I born? Jacksonville, in January of 1950.
    To introduce a question is usually a signal of increasing closeness. In this case it implies that the assumed reader has asked something, is on the scene, and is interested.

Writing for Tone

Where was I born, you ask? Right here in Jacksonville, back in 1950.
    Now the scene is made specific, speaker and reader occupying
the same place ("here"). Another pronoun enters, appealing
directly to the reader's presence.

You ask where I was born? Why, right here in little old Jacksonville.
When? Oh, about 1950.
    Looseness, and cuteness, can be carried to any excess we wish,
so long as we are ready to live with the consequences.

On the following pages, you will find a series of short passages adapted from attempts by undergraduate students, mostly freshmen, to respond to the rewriting exercise described above—"What about your birth and early life?" In each case, the first autobiographical sample was composed in comparative innocence, before the student realized what his subject was about to become—not his own early life, but style. Students were then exposed to a contrast of two pieces of professional reminiscence, illustrating what we have called writer-style and talker-style. In this way the "rules of the game" were worked out in something like the way we have worked them out in our Copperfield/Caulfield analysis. Finally, students were twice invited to rewrite, following first some grammatical-rhetorical patterns of the more formal voice, and then some patterns of an informal persona. In the one case, of course, the assumed reader is kept at a distance, whereas in the second, relations between persona and reader are often very cosy indeed.

§ Some of these students, you will observe, perform their revisions more thoroughly and with more imagination than others do. How could you improve on some of these performances?

1

a. (original version) In March, 1949, I was born as the second child in our family. My sister, five years older than I, had been a war baby, and my parents felt that two children were enough for anyone, thus sealing my fate as the "baby" of the family. Our family circumstances at the time were rather modest; my father was the proprietor of a small business . . .

b. (revision into writer-style) Since my sister, a war baby, had been born five years before I was, and since my parents felt that two children were enough for anyone, when I was born in March 1949 my fate as the "baby" was sealed . . .

c. (revision into talker-style) We weren't exactly the most opulent family at the time. My father—he was a small businessman—owned a service station, and the house we lived in wasn't exactly upper middle-class.

2

a. If I were to mention the number thirteen, most people would immediately shudder because of its superstitious connotation. This notorious number may have proved unlucky for some but in my case it's proved just the opposite, for my family has moved just thirteen times and I consider myself very lucky.

b. The author was warned in one of her younger years about a certain integer which should most definitely be frowned upon and under no circumstances be trusted. This supposedly notorious number has been given the name thirteen. It is the extent of its being notorious, however, which the author wishes to explore. She wonders just how long persons may continue to presume such a viewpoint. In her life span, a total of eighteen years accompanied by thirteen moves, a completely opposite conclusion has been demonstrated.

c. What would be your first reaction if I shouted, "thirteen!"? That's what I thought. You kind of cuddled up in a corner and thought to yourself, "Go away!" Right? Well, I suppose it's a pretty common response. But really, you shouldn't think of it as being so terribly unlucky. Why, in my lifetime "thirteen" has proved to be absolutely great! You see, I've moved that number of times.

3

a. Even though my first name is Kathleen, I like people to call me Kay. I am 17 years old, and I live in Whitesboro, Ohio. I am a Medical Technology major. Someday I hope to work in a hospital as a lab technician.

b. It may be of interest to know that I am a 17-year-old girl, named Kathleen. Whitesboro, Ohio is where I am from. I am a Medical Technology major which I hope will someday lead me into my desired career as a hospital laboratory technician.

c. My first name is Kathleen, but you can call me Kay. I am 17 years old, and I live in Whitesboro, Ohio. Don't be surprised if you've never heard of it, my friends refer to it as a hick town.

Medical Technology is my interest here. One of these days, I hope to be a hospital lab technician.

Chapter 5

Writing for Attitude

With the word *attitude* we refer to relations between the speaker and his subject, how he feels toward what he is talking about. A distinguished critic, I. A. Richards, has used the word *feeling* to denote this relation, and his term may be helpful in suggesting the irrational or emotional aspect of many of our judgments. When we make judgments of value, state likes and dislikes, we are often involved in what are called matters of taste, and about taste, the saying goes, there is no disputing. Actually we dispute constantly about taste. If we do not always do so logically, at least we can recognize how we do go about it, and we can become a little more conscious and cautious in the process. We can observe too, particularly when we encounter irony, how different ways of expressing attitude affect the speaking voice.

Our difficulties in expressing attitudes convincingly are nowhere so obvious as in aesthetic matters, where taste is such a factor. To cite a primitive example, consider the kind of conversation that takes place when an inarticulate but enthusiastic youngster has just come home from the movies.

It was great, Dad.
It was?

Yes, it really was. You should see it.

What was great about it?

Oh, I don't know, the whole thing. The way it was done.

Well, how was it done?

The acting . . . the acting was really terrific. Great cast.

Was it? Who was in it?

Well, I don't remember the names. But really, Dad, it was very good. The story was great too. You should see it.

This ludicrous dialogue may not be so far removed from mature experience as we would like to suppose, for many discussions of attitude between adults are no more informative than this one. Notice that no facts are given about the movie to distinguish it from any other movie—the film in question might have been *Gone with the Wind* or *The Graduate,* for all we can tell from the evidence. To put it another way: For the antecedent of *it* in the conversation, we could freely substitute any title and the conversation would make equally good sense. This is a symptom of a particularly loose—or sloppy—style. It dramatizes a persona whose attention is more on his own feelings than on the object in question. Such a focus is unfortunate if one's purpose is to persuade another individual to adopt an attitude toward a particular thing. On the other hand, it could be just the proper focus if one's purpose is only to convince another of the intensity of one's own feelings.

Another diagram might help. Our scheme for attitude looked this way.

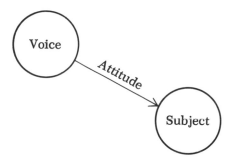

If, however, for the key nouns and pronouns in one's sentences the reader can substitute any of several contrasting and contradictory alternatives, and make equally good sense, then the attitude being expressed is not so much toward the subject as toward the self:

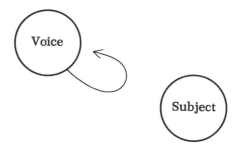

Example:

> —— is more than an extremely competent piece of work. It is an admirable achievement, wrought with skill and sensitivity. The restraint and the refusal to sentimentalize are particularly commendable, contributing to the integrity of the whole. Indeed we might go far before finding a monument to man's contemporary genius the equal of ——.

Parody? Maybe so, but students might apply this test to their own papers on *King Lear,* the art of Picasso, or the Parthenon. If you take out of your sentences the key nouns and substitute ——, is it still perfectly clear what the sentences *have* to be about? If so, you are talking about something, not simply about yourself. In our little encomium above, the subject might be anything at all, vaguely in the aesthetic orbit: a statue, a sonnet, a string quartet. The speaker tells us nothing whatever about what he purports to be talking about; he tells us only a little about himself. His adjectives, "admirable," "commendable," are built from verbs that point to *his* activity: *he* is admiring and commending. Nothing else happens.

Adjectives, and modifiers of adjectives, though necessary, can be symptoms of weakness in expression of attitude. Return to our movie-loving child talking to his dad. His testimony relies almost entirely on adjectives ("great," "terrific") and what are called *intensifiers,* to prop up sagging modifiers ("really," "very"). Overuse of these modifiers can be exceedingly deadly. (Note that adjective and intensifier!) What's the answer; how do we move out of the involuted arrow toward a statement about something?

The answer, of course, is detail.

Well, Dad, it was about John Brown's raid on Harper's Ferry, and the way it was set up, you didn't know whether he was a hero or a nut. There was one zoom shot that showed him picking his teeth, just like anybody, and his speeches sounded like Stokely Carmichael on TV. The soldiers all had bright blue uniforms, must have been a million extras on a wide screen. Lots of shooting. It was great, Dad. You really ought to see it.

This leaves something to be desired, both as credible child talk and as competent film criticism, but at least we begin to learn a little about the subject, and something about the sort of experience that stands behind the asserted attitude. The persona has, to a degree, moved out from his own feelings to some concrete observation.

Our young friend's reliance on adjectives, like "great," is a characteristic of attitudinal writing, as we have said, and a source of weakness. We need to scrutinize adjectives with a wary eye. One way to begin such a scrutiny is to make a simple classification, one we anticipated in Chapter 2. Modifiers like *great, wonderful, fine, terrific,* are of course customarily used to express praise, a favorable attitude. They shed honor on the things modified, and we call them *honorific* adjectives. Then we extend that term to include all language that, in a particular context, expresses a favorable attitude on the part of the speaker. ("Admirable achievement, wrought with skill and sensitivity.") As for unfavorable adjectives (*dreadful, terrible, weak, incompetent, stupid*), and unfavorable language generally, we use the word *pejorative,* the other term in this distinction. Much of our discussion of attitude comes down to decisions about whether language is being used honorifically, or pejoratively, or both, or neither.

And it will already have occurred to the attentive student of style that most of the adjectives listed as examples above might, in certain contexts, be employed for effects quite contrary to those given. For example, in "The Battle Hymn of the Republic" we recall that God's power and authority are alluded to in the phrase "His terrible, swift sword." Here is "terrible" used in the traditional sense of "arousing terror." What is the attitude? Awe, fear? In any event, *not* criticism, disdain, disapproval. (As: "That was a terrible movie," where we have a different attitude and an utterly different persona.) Context, of course, is everything. And the necessity to make decisions about meaning only in the light of contexts becomes especially compelling when we consider a technique of speaking and writing that particularly affects persona and attitude—the technique of *irony*.

Let us hazard a definition in a loose and homemade kind of way. We speak *ironically* when what we seem to be saying points in the opposite direction from what we mean. "What we seem to be saying" refers to the words alone, in crude classifications of meaning such as dictionaries provide, or such as were implied by our honorific-pejorative distinction. When you call something "great," you "seem to be saying" that you approve of it, in accordance with our classification of adjectives. On the other hand, "what we mean" refers to the impact of the language in a context. The two are often in some opposition to each other, to say the least, and when they are, we call the resulting use of language *irony*.

The word *great* will do well enough. It may be that among the young this word is used ironically (that is, pejoratively) more often than it is used straight (honorifically). There is sleet and freezing rain outside; you enter the house and stamp the ice from your clothing. Somebody says, "How's the weather out there?" You have at least these two possible answers:

"It's terrible. Sleet and freezing rain."

"Oh, it's *great!*"

The first, of course, is a *straight* answer; it assumes the questioner desires information, and it gives information accordingly. The voice is serious and matter-of-fact, "sincere."

The second is an ironic answer—crude, perhaps, and all too commonplace, but all the more clearly ironic for that. It expresses attitude only—no other information. Its language implies a suspicion that the questioner spoke ironically too—that he didn't want to find out about the weather (what the words seemed to say), but knew all along exactly what the weather was. (After all, he could see the ice on your clothing.) So he is playing around, as we say, with his question. At any rate, in your answer, you play with a conventionally honorific adjective, making it, partly by your stress and pronunciation, pejorative. You say great, you mean terrible.

In oral speech, we use our physical voice constantly to tip off our listener that we are speaking not straight but ironically.

Writing for Attitude

There is rarely confusion about what we mean—sometimes we reinforce our meaning with gesture, or a smile, just to make sure that we have distinguished between what we "seem to be saying" and what we "really mean." ("Smile when you say that.") Below are some statements of attitude that could be spoken either way. That is, by carefully controlling your vocal chords, you can make these statements mean what they seem to say, or you can make these statements mean just the opposite. Try saying each of these sentences aloud, first straight, then ironically.

Good shot, Jim.

That's some job he did.

Oh we all understood perfectly.

You're a bright one, you are.

What a beautiful piece of scenery.

In actual practice, the surrounding situation will tip off the listener more accurately than the speaker's voice. If Jim has just pitched the ball over the backboard, then "Good shot, Jim" will be ironic no matter how it's uttered. Still, at the risk of overdoing it, you *can* turn on irony with voice alone. Notice, in that last example, what happens to your pronunciation of "beautiful" when you change that normally honorific adjective into an ironic comment. (You might be observing, say, the town dump, or a half-built superhighway: "What a *beautiful* piece of scenery!") There is certainly something you have to do to that adjective, perhaps especially to its first syllable, stressing and elongating the vowel, that signals your ironic meaning to any intelligent listener.

Now let's note what happens to *voice* in the other sense, the created persona who is making the utterance. If we stand, say, on the lip of the Grand Canyon, and we call the scenery beautiful, we are probably speaking like any tourist, and we are certainly saying the obvious. The persona is a bit dull; we become, in the comedian's expression, a "straight man." But if, facing the town dump, we say "beautiful," we become immediately a more complicated person! We may mean the word straight, in which case we are making an interesting and unconventional observation. But we probably mean it ironically, we say what we *don't* mean. This increase in the complexity of the utterance, of the persona making the utterance, is one of the great appeals of irony. It is a way of dramatizing the self as one who doesn't just say the obvious.

But an ironic cry of "Beautiful!" at the town dump is still a pretty simple affair. Let's go back to the Grand Canyon and our original phrasing. "What a beautiful piece of scenery!" Is it possible to utter this statement, in the teeth of the Canyon, ironically? Certainly. But in that case, what is one being ironic about? One is surely not suggesting that the Canyon is ugly. Yet there could be a gap of some sort between what one's words "seem to say" and what the situation actually calls for. The suggestion is that "piece of scenery" is scarcely an adequate phrase for the monumental sight before us, and that "beautiful" is trite. Tourist-talk. The speaker, if he handles his voice skillfully, can be laughing at himself, by implying that his words, or anyone's words, sound silly in the face of such enormous experience. This kind of rueful and sophisticated self-consciousness approaches the keen sense of one's own clichés that we noted in some of Herzog's language in Chapter 3.

Can these ironical turns of phrase, so easily communicated in the spoken language, be translated onto the written page? Of course they can, but it takes some doing to compensate for all the advantages possessed by the speaking voice in action. Instead of elongating the vowel sound to communicate irony ("byoooti-ful"), it is necessary somehow to surround that adjective with other language that will convert the honorific meaning to pejorative.

Mountains of ashes, smouldering. Broken packing boxes with de-cayed oranges, some smashed bedsprings, an overturned bathtub browning in the sun. The rats scurry everywhere. What a beautiful piece of scenery.

In actual practice, of course, an expression of attitude is seldom a choice between "I like it" and "I hate it." What we feel about the town dump is probably some mixture, or perhaps muddle, of horror, amusement, fascination, dismay . . . *All* interesting attitudes are complex. The skillful writer constantly manipulates shadings of honorific and pejorative language, to show his subject as a worthy and complicated experience, and to show himself as a worthy and complicated man.

To review and to summarize some interrelations of tone and attitude, let us return to our Aristotelian diagram of the preceding chapter. But this time we will construct it in a somewhat different form. In respect to tone, let us make horizontal distance between voice and audience symbolize the variations possible. Thus an intimate tone (Hi, How ya been?) might be symbolized thus:

while a more formal tone (How do you do, sir?) might look like this:

As for attitude, let us use vertical relationships to suggest the variations of approval and disdain. In such a scheme, a clearly honorific statement, without irony, would look like this:

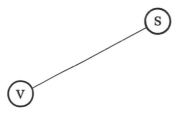

A critical attack, loaded with pejorative language, would then appear in this way:

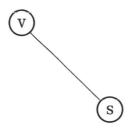

Now with these variations in mind, let us begin with a piece of language that expresses a close relation with audience and an honorific attitude toward subject. As you will recall from our newspaper reading of Chapter 2, there is no better place to look for this particular combination than an advertisement:

1

LOOKING FOR YOUR NEXT MOVE-UP CAR? CONSIDER THE PHOENIX CUSTOM SEDAN. WHY? FOR ITS EXTRA-SPECIAL EXTRAS THAT DON'T COST EXTRA. DISTINCTIVE WRAPAROUND FRONT FENDER LIGHTS. TRIPLE TAILLIGHTS AND BUMPER BACKUP LIGHTS. YOU'LL BE SEEN, COMING AND GOING!

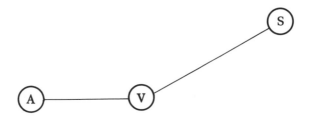

The speaker's character here is warm and friendly. He is a fellow knowledgeable about cars, but he seems to know a lot about you and me, the readers, too. His breezy opening question, his contractions ("don't," "you'll"), his casual sentence fragments and his exclamation point are all devices to secure a close and casual-seeming tone. His attitude, of course, is highly favorable toward the car he is selling, as in most ads.

Now what would happen if we were to try to change that favorable attitude, rewriting the passage so as to produce a criticism of the car's beauties?

2

BEFORE CONSIDERING A PHOENIX CUSTOM SEDAN, IT WOULD BE WISE TO BEWARE OF THE EXCESS LIGHTING AT FRONT AND REAR. YOU WILL PROBABLY FEEL FAR TOO CONSPICUOUS IN SUCH A VEHICLE; THE TRIPLE TAILLIGHTS MAY BE LOOKED UPON AS PARTICULARLY OSTENTATIOUS.

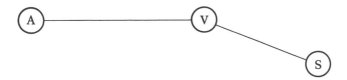

What has happened? In this revision, an attempt to alter the attitude resulted in sharp changes in both voice and tone. The speaker became much less warm and friendly, and in the process of admonishing the reader, he put considerable distance into his tone. His final phrase, "particularly ostentatious," is the sort that we expect to find in fairly formal discourse, where the speaker seems not to pay any direct attention to the reader at all.

Shall we try pushing the passage further in this direction? By removing the "you" from the text, the tone can become even more formal and distant:

3

CONSIDERATION OF A PHOENIX CUSTOM SEDAN PRESENTS THE PUTATIVE OWNER WITH A NUMBER OF UNATTRACTIVE FEATURES, PARTICULARLY THOSE RELATING TO HEADLIGHTS AND TAILLIGHTS. THE SO-CALLED "WRAPAROUND" FRONT FENDERS ADD UP TO LITTLE MORE THAN AN ADDED OSTENTATION.

Among other things, you will note how this fastidious speaker divorces himself from the expression "wraparound," which he considers perhaps a little vulgar, by the familiar device of wrapping it round with quotation marks. But because the speaker is now not warning the reader directly ("beware"), his attitude toward the car is not quite so severe.

In almost all revising, it is impossible to make a change in one element of our triangle without affecting the two others.

Shall we try to bring speaker and reader back together again, while maintaining the critical attitude toward the Phoenix Sedan? We might begin with some irony.

4

YOU'LL LOVE IT, ALL RIGHT. ALL THAT SHOW-OFF LIGHTING, FORE AND AFT. YOU'LL FEEL LIKE A SHOWBOAT DRIVING DOWN THE STREET IN THAT NEW PHOENIX—TRIPLE TAILLIGHTS YET!

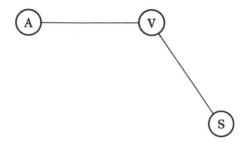

What has happened now? We have brought reader and speaker closer together, to be sure, by such translations as "ostentation" into "show-off." But inevitably this changes the speaker's attitude as well! The poor Phoenix has sunk even lower on our diagram, in response to the language. And the character of the speaker, of course, has undergone violent change in the direction of casual oral speech, slanginess, a fellow ready to exaggerate in dramatic style as we do in conversations with close friends.

Notice that as we have varied our speakers, tones, and attitudes, the very genre or kind of writing changes. These little passages have implied contexts—places where you might expect to see such things. The original ad (see 1), for example, was simply plucked from a magazine, and it looks right at home there. Version 4 might possibly appear in a letter to a very personal friend—it is hard to imagine where else it could appear in written English, except perhaps inside quotation marks in a novel.

Now can we seek a neutral attitude toward the car? Observe what happens to the character of the speaker, the tone, and the genre, in this effort:

5

UPWARD MOBILITY IN AMERICA IS OFTEN ACCOMPANIED BY SUCCESSIVE PURCHASES OF NEW AUTOMOBILES. IN MANY GROUPS SOCIAL STATUS MAY BE SYMBOLIZED BY SUCH DESIR-ABLE FEATURES AS DISTINCTIVE HEADLIGHTS OR MULTIPLE TAILLIGHTS IN "CUSTOM" MODELS.

Here is the social scientist talking, of course, and his medium is the textbook, or learned article. Notice that here the car (or "automobile," as he puts it) has become an example of a larger, and abstract, phenomenon like social mobility or status. The speaker can then adopt the familiar "objective" attitude toward a symptom of culture, treating it as a scientist might an observation of nature. (You may doubt, though, whether he has quite avoided a value-judgment.) As for the reader, he is kept at a distance, as he often is when people are considered in large groups and when objects are considered as examples of abstract concepts.

For practice in manipulating tone and attitude on your own, you might select an ad that appeals to you and rewrite to conform to several different relationships among our three variables. In each case, add a sentence or two describing the character of the speaker you have created, and speculating as to the *genre* you have exemplified. That is, where (if anywhere), and under what circumstances, might you be likely to find a piece of prose like the one you have just perpetrated?

Here are some possibilities:

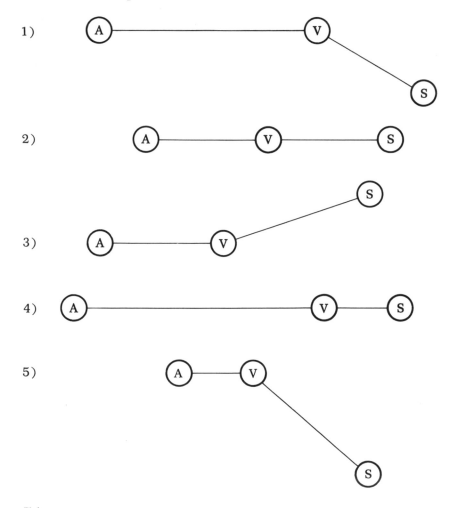

Writing for Attitude

§ Having played this game with an ad, you can of course go on to play similar games with other kinds of attitudinal statements, including the most serious and respectable. Some further possibilities: a descriptive statement about a college campus, from the college catalog; a remark on the State of the Union, from the President; or a definition of the meaning of life, from your favorite philosopher. Who knows—you may find yourself improving some of these estimable voices. In any case, you will be having some practice trying out your own.

Chapter 6

Language and Role-Playing

We have been speaking in this book about role-playing, suggesting that practice in taking on a role not necessarily your own is a useful kind of experience. Useful in what way? First, there is a practical or pedagogical motive having to do with sheer skill and fluency in writing. It seems plausible that writers who have enjoyed a wide range of involvement in composition, who have played many stylistic roles, can operate more effectively as they encounter the sundry verbal challenges that life offers them. Analogies with other fields of endeavor may be helpful. The concert musician, during his training, learns something about many instruments as well as a great deal about one. The physicist performs at times as mathematician, as chemist, as engineer. It is a truism that one knows more about one's own language after one has studied a foreign language. Who knows English who only English knows? By experimenting with many variations of persona, tone, and attitude, the student can presumably approach any single problem of expression more confidently and successfully. That at any rate is one assumption of this book.

But to say this much is to argue for little more than a kind of technical facility, important though that is. After all, we are concerned finally with becoming more than a sort of linguistic chameleon, changing styles at the drop of anybody's hat. A further assumption of this book, then, is that role-playing is one approach to self-discovery. We can learn who we are by learning who we can be or might be. There is an oft-quoted remark made by writers that is not a joke, though it sounds like one: "How do I know what I mean until I've said it?" Similarly, how do we know who we are until we try ourselves in action, acting out various parts? The word *act*, as we have said, like many words from drama, carries double significance. We act, seriously and vigorously, as human beings in a real world. We act, also and at the same time, in a dramatic sense, by creating for ourselves a role to play, a performance to act out. The word *performance*, as we noted in our opening chapter, conveys a similar doubleness, for our performance as role-player is precisely our effort to perform well in the face of all life's vicissitudes.

There is nothing new in this. In the present chapter we will illustrate with brief quotations some positions of others towards role-playing and voice, suggesting that through role-playing we may "come to terms" with our very selves.

We begin with a forthright statement about role-playing taken from the magazine *Science*, an unlikely source, you might suppose, to be concerned with such matters.

> In our society we speak as we live: according to our roles. Our roles are many, and the ways we use speech are as numerous. One may be a physicist, gardener, husband, father, lover, do-it-yourselfer . . . birder, surfer, hiker, biker, piker, Scout leader, discussion-group chairman, and much more, and all more or less contemporaneously and with no trouble at all. And each of these roles requires a different use of language if the role-player is "with it."[1]

To the social scientist, especially the sociologist, the expression "role theory" has become commonplace. Here is a formulation that will sound familiar to readers of this book.

> It is probably no mere historical accident that the word person, in its first meaning, is a mask. It is rather a recognition of the fact that everyone is always and everywhere, more or less consciously, playing

a role . . . It is in these roles that we know each other, it is in these roles that we know ourselves.

In a sense, and in so far as this mask represents the conception we have formed of ourselves—the role we are striving to live up to—this mask is our truer self, the self we would like to be. In the end, our conception of our role becomes second nature and an integral part of our personality. We come into the world as individuals, achieve character, and become persons.[2]

Another sociologist, Erving Goffman, has attempted to explain much of human interaction in terms of metaphors from the theatre. His book, *The Presentation of Self in Everyday Life,* argues that, from the point of view of the student of performances, it may not make a great difference whether one is examining a role that is "honest" or "dishonest."

We come . . . to a realization that while the performance offered by imposters and liars is quite flagrantly false and differs in this respect from ordinary performances, both are similar in the care their performers must exert in order to maintain the impression that is fostered. Thus, for example, we know that the formal code of British civil servants and of American baseball umpires obliges them not only to desist from making improper "deals" but also to desist from innocent action which might possibly give the (wrong) impression that they are making deals. Whether an honest performer wishes to convey the truth or whether a dishonest performer wishes to convey a falsehood, both must take care to enliven their performances with appropriate expressions, exclude from their performances expressions that might discredit the impression being fostered, and take care lest the audience impute unintended meanings. Because of these shared dramatic contingencies, we can profitably study performances that are quite false in order to learn about ones that are quite honest.[3]

But no one, of course, including Mr. Goffman, would want to argue that a fraudulent performance is as worthy as an honest one, and indeed we may quite properly feel some very concrete dangers in the whole prospect of life as drama. If every expression is an "act," and if one is to be self-conscious about one's own actor-role, then is one not inhibited from saying loudly and clearly what one really means? Or ought to mean? At least one critic, Benjamin DeMott, has complained that among teachers especially there appears, in an atmosphere of drama-consciousness, a weak-kneed "academic noncombativeness."

The holiday ideology of taste, with its eschewal of direct summary or crystallization, is actually a consequence of the revolution in the name of the dramatic that was fought and won generations ago in high culture. But the noncommercial inheritors of that revolution, men who regard it as a stroke for truth rather than for profit, are themselves as fully in its thrall—which is to say, as wary of crystallization—as are the men of commerce. On elevated grounds they have turned hostility to the didactic or non-dramatic view of life into a positive value; they see the summarizing critic, the man who attempts to translate a story or poem from its own terms into those of moral discourse, as one who dishonors the shrine of Art.[4]

We can grant this danger—and others—in a vision of the world as a field for dramatic action. It nevertheless remains that learning by role-playing is a fundamental activity in education. During the summer of 1966, at Dartmouth College, a prestigious group of British and American teachers of English met in a seminar to confer on their common problems. Their report makes much of role-playing from the very earliest grades: note the introduction of our term *voice:*

By assuming a role—taking on a stance, setting up a model—a child is trying out a version of himself and his possibilities without committing himself permanently, and as in story-telling or poem-making is both choosing and laying a basis for future choices of personality and values.

The taking on of dramatic roles, the dramatic encounter with new situations and with new possibilities of the self, is not something we *teach* children but something they bring to school for us to help them develop. Their play reminds us—if only we observe—that our verbally dominated college culture takes in only part of life and, carried into school, confuses and even repels children without our verbal confidence. To help pupils encounter life as it is, the complexity of relationships in a group and dynamic situation, there is nothing more direct and simple that we can offer them than drama. . . .

As drama develops, the learning becomes more complex. Pupils of fourteen to eighteen learn to change and reverse roles, to see the situation from many perspectives, and—in the work of writing scripts

—to use the many voices of the "characters" to build within themselves an image of the complexity of the world as they know it. Preceding the scripts and developing through them is a new discipline of interpretation, of seeing more than one way of "reading" a situation. To work on a scene is to realize the complexity of human feelings and attitudes. Thus drama makes explicit the variousness of life, but also acknowledges its elusiveness. The best scripts remind us that "Your good writer is your wide and various man: a character nicely conscious of the elements of personhood excluded by this or that act of writing and ever in a half-rage to allude to them: to hint at characterological riches even where these can't be spent."[5]

That last quoted remark, illuminating and suggestive, was made by the aforesaid Mr. DeMott, who was one of the conferees at Dartmouth. The Seminar's report goes on to indicate some of the limitations of the written language, as against live "drama," limitations we are becoming particularly aware of in an age of film and television.

"Drama" means doing, acting things out rather than working on them in abstract and in private. When possible it is the truest form of learning, for it puts knowledge and understanding to their test in action. A book is an inadequate medium for the discussion of drama and talk: one cannot present work in progress in all its immediacy. But suppose a film had been made, rather than a book, to report our Seminar's version of English. Drama and talk would then have been central, with writing and reading in the background somewhere. The medium shapes the message (as with language). This important caveat has two implications. First, work at the centres for curriculum development in English needs to incorporate film and television, radio and sound recording, for otherwise drama and talk will tend to be neglected in discussions there. (B.B.C. television has more than once shown the possibilities of the medium for discussing improvised drama.) Second, the centres themselves need to become English workshops where, at their own level, teachers are encouraged to talk, act, write and give recitals of readings, to sustain and develop their insight into similar work with pupils.[6]

The impact of electronic media on our ways of seeing and communicating has received enormous and deserved publicity in recent years, most notoriously in the works of Marshall McLuhan. A distinguished Jesuit literary critic, Walter J. Ong, much influenced by McLuhan, has written widely on what happens to a culture when it turns "oral-aural" rather than print-minded and visual. A rather long quotation (from his book, *The Barbarian Within*) is appropriate.

Heightening the oral-aural element in a culture does much more than merely de-emphasize vision. It subtly heightens the personalist element in a culture. For the plenary development of sound, the human voice, is a manifestation of the person. Even more than it is a manifestation of an understanding of objects, speech is a calling of one person to another, of an interior to an interior. Sight presents always surfaces, presents even depth as a lamination of surfaces, whereas sound presents always interiors, for sound is impossible without some resonance. The post-Baconian preoccupation with sight and "observation" produced the world of Enlightenment, a world of objects and things without convincing personal presences, giving us the strangely silent universe which Newtonian physics and Deism both supposed. Printing was the harbinger of this Newtonian world, for printing is spectacularly allied with surface or "object" treatment of reality. Picasso's collages use bits of printed posters or newspapers to establish a sense of flat surface because print is sensed as indissolubly allied with surface. Scraps of printing in the collages serve precisely the function of returning the eye from the perspective depths in other parts of the assemblage to the plane surface of the painting—it is unconvincing to imagine print on anything other than something relatively flat and smooth.

Strangely enough, although it is in part a visualist development, television has moved away from this effect of print. It has been a personalizing, not an objectifying, medium. The discussion panel, with its interchange of personalities, is properly a television phenomenon. Such personal interchange was difficult to manage on radio, for there individual persons could only with difficulty be kept distinct. Hence the use of voice was not brought to its fullest fruition. By the same token television is a more feasible means of education than radio. This is not because it can use visual aid devices (figures written on a blackboard on television cannot be seen by any viewer unless the camera is turned on them—they lack the permanent availability of figures on a classroom blackboard). It is because television better implements personal rapport between instructor and student.

But television is not the only manifestation of the growing interest in the human person which accompanies the resurgence of voice in our culture. Another manifestation is the self-conscious personalism of our times. The twentieth century, from one point of view the most mechanized of all ages of mankind, is from another point of view the most personalized. No other age has generated a whole philosophy of personalism such as one finds in the works of Martin Buber, Gabriel Marcel, and others. At a much less reflective, more superficial, and nevertheless significant level, no civilization before our technological civilization has given such attention to problems of personnel and personality in matters even of industrial performance. The "I" and the "thou" have never been the objects of more explicit treatment than now. In the future, alongside the digital and analogue computers and other mathematicizing developments such as Western culture has specialized in more and more over the past few hundred years, the human person will receive more and more attention, not in every quarter but in significant milieus and ways. . . .

It is through awareness of the paramount role of voice in human activity that students of English or of any other language today must seek to understand the reactivation of the oral-aural element in human culture. Voice is coming into its own as never before. But the ways in which it is doing so, and the elements in our culture which favor voice as well as those which militate against it, are complex in the extreme. We can arm ourselves and our students only by vigilant awareness of what is going on about us. In particular, teachers and students of language and literature must cultivate sensitivity to the more profound significance of the media of popular culture—which is not the same thing as either uncritical acceptance of popular culture or entrenched hostility to all its manifestations. Any kind of genuine sensitivity to literature of any age or culture has become thoroughly impossible unless a person has grown seriously, not phrenetically— reflective about contemporary communications media. Men today— and, above all, high school, college and university students—live en-globed in a universe of sound emanating from radio and hi-fi sets which surpasses anything any earlier human culture has known, both in the total decibel output at any given moment and in incessancy. Reflection on the condition of the new media and the changes they are effecting in human life will probably produce no pat formulae either to describe the totality of the present situation or to prescribe highly simplified lines of action. But it should enable us to live.[7]

But role-playing has been going on a long time, of course, and the student might ponder the situation, familiar to anthropologists, in which the actor and the character being acted become almost indistinguishable. Such is apparently the case in primitive cultures when, for instance, the dancer in the magic ceremony plays the role of an animal. The following paragraph is from a book by a cultural historian, Johan Huizinga, called *Homo Ludens: A Study of the Play Element in Culture.*

When a certain form of religion accepts a sacred identity between two things of a different order, say a human being and an animal, this relationship is not adequately expressed by calling it a "symbolical" correspondence as *we* conceive this. The identity, the essential oneness of the two goes far deeper than the correspondence between a substance and its symbolic image. It is a mystic unity. The one has *become* the other. In his magic dance the savage *is* a kangaroo. We must always be on our guard against the deficiencies and differences of our means of expression. In order to form any idea at all of the mental habits of the savage we are forced to give them in our terminology. Whether we will or not we are always transposing the savage's ideas of religion into the strictly logical modes of our own thought. We express the relationship between him and the animal he "identifies" himself with, as a "being" for him but a "playing" for us. He has taken on the "essence" of the kangaroo, says the savage; he is playing the kangaroo, say we. The savage, however, knows nothing of the conceptual distinctions between "being" and "playing"; he knows nothing of "identity," "image," or "symbol." Hence it remains an open question whether we do not come nearest to the mental attitude of the savage performing a ritual act, by adhering to this primary, universally understandable term "play." In play as we conceive it the distinction between belief and make-believe breaks down. . . . By considering the whole sphere of so-called primitive culture as a play-sphere we pave the way to a more direct and more general understanding of its peculiarities than any meticulous psychological or sociological analysis would allow.[8]

In this book we have scarcely confronted directly the problem of how the writer himself relates to the role he plays through his style. What is the connection between these two "characters"? For Walt Whitman, the difference between the man himself and his style was obvious. "The greatest poet has less a marked style," he wrote, "and is more the free channel of himself. He says to his art, I will not be meddlesome, I will not have in my writing any elegance or effect or originality to hang in the way between me and the rest like curtains. I will have nothing hang in the way, not the richest curtains. What I tell I tell for precisely what it is." To this, literary critic Susan Sontag has responded as follows:

83

By likening style to a curtain, he has of course confused style with decoration and for this would be speedily faulted by most critics. To conceive of style as a decorative encumbrance on the matter of the work suggests that the curtain could be parted and the matter revealed; or, to vary the metaphor slightly, that the curtain could be rendered transparent. But this is not the only erroneous implication of the metaphor. What the metaphor also suggests is that style is a matter of more or less (quantity), thick or thin (density). And, though less obviously so, this is just as wrong as the fancy that an artist possess the genuine option to have or not to have a style. Style is not quantitative, any more than it is superadded. A more complex stylistic convention—say, one taking prose further away from the diction and cadences of ordinary speech—does not mean that the work has "more" style.

Indeed, practically all metaphors for style amount to placing matter on the inside, style on the outside. It would be more to the point to reverse the metaphor. The matter, the subject, is on the outside; the style is on the inside. As Cocteau writes: "Decorative style has never existed. Style is the soul, and unfortunately with us the soul assumes the form of the body." Even if one were to define style as the manner of our appearing, this by no means necessarily entails an opposition between a style that one assumes and one's "true" being. In fact, such a disjunction is extremely rare. In almost every case, our manner of appearing *is* our manner of being. The mask is the face.[9]

To Father Ong again, role-playing and voice are the very qualities that make us and keep us human. Here is the paragraph from which the quotation on our frontispiece was untimely ripped:

Actors are real persons, but they perform not as the persons they are, but as persons they are not. They have at times worn masks, to show that they are not themselves, but something other. Yet, is it not highly indicative that the word for mask, *persona* (that-through-which-the-sound-comes), has given both to the ancients and to us the word for person? It is as though this ability to take on the role of another shows the actor's own humanity, shows that the other is already within him, and is, indeed, the shadow of his most real self. Ortega y Gasset points out that the brute animal is pure *alteración*, pure "otheration," in the sense that he cannot enter into himself—and yet, by the same token, he can find in himself and recognize by contrast the echoes of the personal other, the "thou," the alienation or *alteración* which is there. Thus acting a role, realizing in a special way one's identity (in a sense) with a someone who (in another sense) one is not, remains one of the most human things a man can do. No brute animal can act a role. Unable to recognize himself, he finds it impossible to recognize what by contrast with self is other. By the same token, he has nothing against which to set a role so that it is a role.[10]

We end this little collection with a contemporary of Whitman's who urges us to take high ground in our search for a voice. Here is Thoreau with a well-known word of advice for all writers of compositions:

It is a ridiculous demand which England and America make, that you should speak so that they can understand you. Neither men nor toadstools grow so. As if that were important, and there were not enough to understand you without them. As if Nature could support but one order of understandings, could not sustain birds as well as quadrupeds, flying as well as creeping things, and *hush* and *whoa*, which Bright can understand, were the best English. As if there were safety in stupidity alone. I fear chiefly lest my expression may not be *extra-vagant* enough, may not wander far enough beyond the narrow limits of my daily experience, so as to be adequate to the truth of which I have become convinced. *Extra vagance!* It depends on how you are yarded. The migrating buffalo, which seeks new pastures in another latitude, is not extravagant like the cow which kicks over the pail, leaps the cowyard fence, and runs after her calf, in milking time. I desire to speak somewhere *without* bounds; like a man in a waking moment, to men in their waking moments; for I am convinced that I cannot exaggerate enough to lay the foundation of a true expression. Who that has heard a strain of music feared then lest he should speak extravagantly any more forever? In view of the future or possible, we should live quite laxly and undefined in front, our outlines dim and misty on that side; as our shadows reveal an insensible perspiration toward the sun. The volatile truth of our words should continually betray the inadequacy of the residual statement. The truth is instantly *translated;* its literal monument alone remains. The words which express our faith and piety are not definite; yet they are significant and fragrant like frankincense to superior natures.[11]

If you were to write a final paper in response to this book, it could be centered on what has certainly become in our time a fashionable topic: the nature of personal identity. But try limiting the approach, at least on this occasion, to a consideration of those very exercises in role-playing that you have already undergone in this book. No doubt there are many ways to express identity besides suffering a teacher's games with language. All the same, in preparation for *this* final paper, let us review a list of principal exercises that the conscientious student of this book has now performed:

> From Chapter 1, page 10. Rewritings of various famous opening passages employing a first-person-singular voice.

> From Chapter 2, page 26. Your very own newspaper, with its political column, social news, editorial, letters, sports, TV review, and so on.

> From Chapter 3, page 41. A gathering of letters: to your congressman, your milkman, your broker, your girlfriend or boyfriend, your roommate, and your roommate's mother.

> From Chapter 4, page 57. Three different versions of your birth and early life, as told in different styles.

> From Chapter 5, page 74. Five statements manipulating voice, tone, and attitude in accordance with an assortment of diagrams.

§ Now consider a remark made at the beginning of Chapter 6. "Through role-playing we may 'come to terms' with our very selves." Is this true? Does it have any meaning in your own experience, as you have responded to the exercises in this book? You could approach such questions, first, by reviewing carefully your own varied personas in those passages you composed. Some of them, no doubt, seem closer to the "real you" than others. Which ones? Which ones are you proudest of, and why? Are they the ones that also seem to speak for *you* most directly?

§ Who is this *you* who is or is not accurately expressed in the roles you have played in these exercises? Can you compose a paragraph that does accurately express the real you? If you can't, why can't you? What is difficult about this?

86

Language and Role-Playing

§ Finally, how does one "come to terms" with oneself? What terms? Is the word "terms" here actually a synonym for "means of expression"? If so, what terms are particularly worth study, so that you may come to "know thyself"?

Your paper, then, will finally address itself to that notorious imperative of many centuries' standing. What does it mean, what do you have to do, to Know Thyself?

There is an old musician's joke about a young violinist, fiddlecase under his arm, who emerges bewildered from a New York subway. Approaching an older man also carrying an instrument, he asks, "How do I get to Carnegie Hall?"

The answer is, "Practice."

Sources of Quoted Passages
and Notes

Chapter 1

1. Daniel Defoe, *Robinson Crusoe* (1719).

2. Laurence Sterne, *Tristram Shandy* (1760).

3. Samuel Butler, *The Way of All Flesh* (1903).

4. Mark Twain, *A Connecticut Yankee in King Arthur's Court* (1889).

5. Gertrude Stein, *The Autobiography of Alice B. Toklas* (New York: Random House, 1954).

6. Saul Bellow, *The Adventures of Augie March* (New York: Viking Press, 1954).

7. Jack Kerouac, *On the Road* (New York: Viking Press, 1957).

8. S. J. Perelman, *The Road to Miltown* (New York: Simon and Schuster, 1957).

9. John Barth, *Giles Goat-Boy* (Garden City, N.Y.: Doubleday, 1967).

10. Dylan Thomas, *Quite Early One Morning* (New York: New Directions, 1954), p. 3.

11. *Ibid.*, p. 20.

12. Dylan Thomas, "Fern Hill," *Selected Writings* (New York: New Directions, 1946).

Chapter 3

1. Virginia Woolf, *Mrs. Dalloway* (New York: Harcourt, Brace and Company, 1925).
2. William Faulkner, "Barn Burning," *Collected Stories* (New York: Random House, 1950).
3. Anthony Trollope, *The Eustace Diamonds* (1872).
4. James Joyce, *Ulysses* (New York: Random House, 1934).
5. Theodore Dreiser, *Sister Carrie* (1900).
6. Aldous Huxley, *Point Counter-Point* (1928).
7. George Eliot, *Middlemarch* (1872).
8. Frederick Buechner, *A Long Day's Dying* (New York: Alfred A. Knopf, 1950).
9. Flannery O'Connor, *A Good Man Is Hard to Find* (New York: Harcourt, Brace and World, 1955).
10. Elizabeth Bowen, *The Little Girls* (New York: Alfred A. Knopf, 1963).

Chapter 6

1. Arnold B. Larson, in *Science*, 139 (January 18, 1963), 245–246.
2. Robert Ezra Park, *Race and Culture* (Glencoe, Ill.: The Free Press, 1950), p. 249.
3. Erving Goffman, *The Presentation of Self in Everyday Life* (Garden City, N.Y.: Doubleday Anchor Books, 1959), p. 66.
4. Benjamin DeMott, *You Don't Say* (New York: Harcourt, Brace and World, 1966), p. 214.
5. John Dixon, *Growth Through English* (Reading, Eng.: National Association for the Teaching of English, 1967), pp. 37–39.
6. *Ibid.*, p. 43.
7. Walter J. Ong, S. J., *The Barbarian Within* (New York: Macmillan, 1962), pp. 225–227, 229.
8. Johan Huizinga, *Homo Ludens* (Boston: Beacon Press, 1955), p. 25.
9. Susan Sontag, *Against Interpretation* (New York: Farrar, Straus & Giroux, 1966), pp. 18–19.
10. Ong, *op. cit.*, p. 54.
11. H. D. Thoreau, *Walden* (1854).